EXPLORING BADENOCH

Clan Macpherson Country

JOHN BARTON

CLAN MACPHERSON MUSEUM TRUST

To Heera
for all her encouragement

Exploring Badenoch
Clan Macpherson Country

Contents   Page

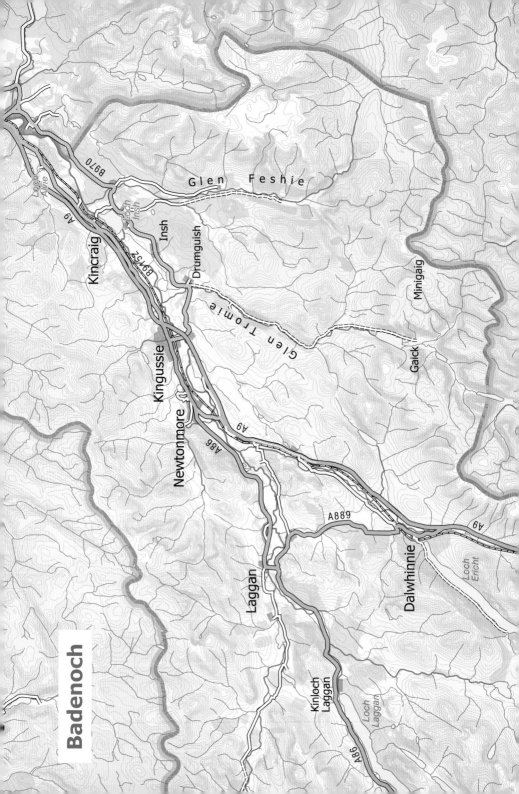

Chapter 1
Introduction

Where shall we go today?

This book is for visitors and for residents of Badenoch who wish to find out a little more about their immediate surroundings. By using the public bus services, it is possible to visit many of the places around Newtonmore and Kingussie, and beyond Kincraig, but a car or bicycle is the only practical means of transport if it is intended to explore the more distant roads. Indeed a bicycle is more than desirable for the private roads in Glen Feshie, Glen Tromie and Ardverikie.

Badenoch is a district of Inverness-shire (now part of Highland Region) a little more than half way between Perth and Inverness, and comprises the parishes of Laggan, Kingussie, Insh and Alvie. The area largely corresponds with the catchment area of the upper River Spey, together with its principal tributaries, the Feshie, the Tromie, the Truim and the Calder; but it is significant that the parish of Laggan extends midway down Loch Ericht (which ultimately flows into the Tay), and the same parish also includes Loch Laggan – the source of the River Spean, which flows west until it reaches the Great Glen. To the east, the parish of Alvie extends on the left bank of the Spey, almost as far as the present town of Aviemore; and on the right bank to the boundary between Inshriach and Rothiemurchus Estates.

The alignment of the main road through Badenoch tempts one to think of the area as having a north/south aspect, but a quick glance at a map will show that the River Spey largely flows through the district in a west to east direction; and that Newtonmore and Laggan lie to the west of Kingussie. It is accordingly this orientation which has been adopted in giving directions throughout this book.

With the exception of Forestry Commission property, practically all the lands of Badenoch are in private ownership. Scotland has always been fortunate in that it has never been a criminal offence to wander over private land. However, walkers were sometimes exposed to verbal abuse of a most threatening nature. Since the passing of the "Freedom to Roam" legislation in 2003, such incidents should not now occur. There is also an "Access Code" which is frequently referred to, but it is rarely set out in full - as it seeks to cover every possible contingency. Stalking for red deer stags is permitted from 1 July to 20 October; and the stalking for hinds is permitted from the latter date through to 15 February. One may still come across a notice with this information and that high velocity rifles will be used – giving the impression that you will be in mortal danger if you pass that point in the second half of the year. For roe deer, the seasons for bucks and does cover all 12 months in the year. In practice, grouse beating and deer stalking only take place on any particular area over a few days in any year, and such is the necessary accuracy in shooting that there has never been any record of a hill walker being hit by a stray shot. Where a "shoot" is to take place, it is immediately apparent by the collection of estate vehicles at the end of the road, and the average person will choose to vary their plans and find a peaceful place elsewhere.

In early times, it was customary for drovers to be accompanied by their dogs, and these dogs provided an essential service in keeping the cattle moving to their destination. In exercising the freedom to roam, it is permissible to be accompanied by your dog, but great caution should be taken when sheep are in lamb, or cattle have calves – as there have been occasions when cattle have attacked a dog and its owner, sometimes with fatal results. Also, on the open moor, during May and June, dogs can often disturb ground nesting birds.

Traditionally, the heart of the Clan Macpherson has been in Badenoch, and especially centred around the estate of Cluny in Laggan. Until 1932, successive chiefs and their families resided at Cluny; and although the present Chief does not reside there, he is still known as "Macpherson of Cluny" or simply as "Cluny". The low point in the Clan was in 1746 after the last Jacobite Rising, when Cluny House was set on fire, the Estates were confiscated and there was a price of one thousand guineas (£1050) for the capture of Cluny. He remained in hiding in Badenoch for nine years before escaping to France. The Estates were restored to his son in 1782 and he built the present Cluny Castle. Sadly, the Estates were found to be insolvent after the last resident member of the Cluny family died in 1932. The Castle and all its contents, including all the historical relics, were sold.

But out of this last tragedy, a "phoenix" arose. All the important relics were purchased by enthusiastic clansmen, the Clan Macpherson Association was formed in 1947, and by 1952 the Association had raised sufficient funds to acquire the present Museum building in Newtonmore. Since then, the Museum has been greatly expanded and it is open to visitors every day throughout the Summer. The Association has also gone from strength to strength with active Branches wherever Macphersons have settled abroad; and in the first weekend of August, a large number of clansmen gather in Badenoch for their annual Rally, which includes an impressive March over the Spey to the Highland Games at Newtonmore.

For those interested in serious walking or climbing, there are already a number of available books and pamphlets. A comprehensive list of walks, with helpful information and supporting maps can also be found at www.walkhighlands.co.uk. Nevertheless, a supplementary paragraph has been added to each chapter with information about paths of particular interest. Most of these walks extend to about 4 to 5 miles, and should not take more than two to three hours.

Map number 35 in the Ordnance Survey Landranger series (on a scale of 1:50 000), covers practically the whole of Badenoch; or there is the alternative of maps OL55, OL56 and OL57 in the Explorer series at a scale of 1:25 000.

Long distant walks

1) The Speyside Way, begins/ends at Buckie on the Moray Firth. In September 2015, it was extended from Aviemore to Kincraig; and at the time of writing, there are active plans for a further extension, broadly following the line of the existing Badenoch Way on to Kingussie.

2) The East Highland Way (from Fort William to Aviemore) does not have "official" status but provides a route from Loch Laggan.
Details of both of these routes can be found at www.walkhighlands.co.uk

Mackenzie Fountain, Kingussie

Chapter 2
Kingussie Walk

Kingussie has had three separate lives. In the beginning, it was the location of the Parish Church, with the principal township of the parish at Ruthven - on the other side of the Spey.

There is a tradition within the Clan Macpherson that some time in the 12th century, Muriach, the historical parson of Kingussie, on the death of his brother without issue, became head of his family and succeeded to the chieftainship of Clan Chattan. It is said that in 1173, Muriach obtained a dispensation from the Pope and married a daughter of the Thane of Cawder. (There is no trace of this dispensation in the Vatican!) Gillichattan was the eldest son and the second son was Ewen, from whom are descended the Cluny Macphersons (the hereditary chiefs of the Clan Macpherson). A charter of 25 August 1203 by William the Lion in favour of the Bishop of Moray referred to the church at Kingussie.

It is recorded in the (First) Statistical Account of Scotland (1798) – written by the parish minister – that "sheep farming has not yet made any considerable progress in the parish, because the wool that could have been manufactured in the place, must be sent by a long land carriage to buyers" elsewhere. Significantly, the writer added that "the flax that might have proved a source of wealth to both proprietor and tacksman (tenant farmer), has been neglected, because skilled people are not collected in one close neighbourhood, to carry it through the whole process".

These comments may have influenced the Duke of Gordon. In 1799, he laid out the new town of Kingussie; and, taking advantage of the plentiful water of the River Gynack, he established a mill with a view to using the local flax for the manufacture of linen. The mill was not a success and further mills were set up for the carding, spinning and waulking of the local wool. The parish minister, in his contribution to the New Statistical Account of Scotland (1835) writes that -

"the parish contains two inns, and ten or eleven alehouses, - the effects of which, especially of the alehouses, upon the morals of the people, are certainly of a pernicious tendency."

And a guide book published in 1850 describes Kingussie as -

"having no trade or manufactures, and yet possessing a large pauperized population, chiefly thrown in upon it by the successive clearings of the adjoining districts... the inhabitants are now entirely dependent for employment on the neighbouring corn and sheep farmers... Among the privations of the poor people the scarcity of fuel is often severely felt in winter, as some of the most accessible peat mosses are nearly exhausted, and the cost of carting coals so far inland is beyond their means; yet, we regret to say, that the consumption of whisky here, and in all the Highland villages, is most inordinate and disgraceful."

Eleven years later, Queen Victoria referred to Kingussie as "a very straggling place with very few cottages." Her experience there was of -

"a small, curious, chattering crowd of people – who, however, did not really make us out, but evidently suspected who we were. Grant and Brown kept them off the carriages, and gave them evasive answers, directing them to the wrong carriage, which was most amusing. One old gentleman, with a high wide-awake, was especially inquisitive."

It was two years later, in September 1863, that there was the biggest change, when the railway was opened. (Originally known as the Inverness & Perth Junction Railway, it became the Highland Railway in 1865).

It is appropriate, therefore that we should begin at the station. George T Hay, in his *Perth and North Thereof* (1966) describes his early memory, probably dating back to the last years of the 19th century.

"When we reached Kingussie it was evening and the station lamps were lit. There hungry passengers rushed to the refreshment-room for food or a dram to fortify them for the long miles ahead over Dava Moor. Only the gentry remained in their compartments, to which valets and ladies' maids brought dinner-baskets ordered in advance. At Kingussie, too, the train's oil-lamps were lit amid a furious banging of trapdoors on the carriage roofs, through which was thrust, frequently without result, a smoky rag-torch."

The reason for the relatively long stop at Kingussie was that the steam engines required to take on a prodigious quantity of water which was conveyed by a large diameter flexible hose. As a boy, it was always fascinating to see the flood of water when the hose was detached from the engine tender. Also within living memory was the bookstall and the goods yard with turn-table. The early trains required a lower platform. To this day, the platform on the south side of the station has never been raised, and step boxes are placed in this platform at strategic intervals to assist passengers on the rare occasions that this platform is used.

In September 1873, Queen Victoria alighted at Kingussie Station en route to Inverlochy Castle in Lochaber. She was welcomed by Old Cluny, the then Chief of the Clan Macpherson, and there were two triumphal arches and other decorations.

At the entrance to the station square, there is a tall fountain for watering the cattle and horses that used to be led from the town to the common grazings on the other side of the railway. Peter Alexander Cameron Mackenzie was born in Kingussie on the 12th August 1856. He travelled extensively, particularly in South America, on behalf of the Singer Manufacturing Company, of which his uncle was President. In 1894 the King of Portugal, Dom Carlos made Peter Mackenzie a Viscount for services to the Portuguese people living in Brazil, and he was made a Count two years later - the Count de Serra Largo. In 1911, Peter Mackenzie donated funds to build the fountain. He also built many other buildings in Kingussie, and was chieftain of Kingussie Shinty Club for 34 years until his death in 1931.

Leaving the station square, one may wish to pause at the bridge where Spey Street crosses the River Gynack. The original stream was described by a Dr Sinton as winding its way through the flat occupied by the Free Church and the Railway Station, in the natural and picturesque fashion that might be expected of a Highland burn. However, the course of the river was straightened when the railway was built in 1863, to increase the clearance under the railway bridge. Notwithstanding, the Gynack still floods from time to time; and a careful examination of the road bridge will show that the iron railings are detachable so that floodwater can, if necessary, flow over the road.

Thereafter it is a pleasant walk through the Memorial Garden, up to the Duke of Gordon Hotel. In 1838, about 20 houses were demolished to allow the building of the Hotel - then known as the Gordon Arms Hotel. Lord Cockburn, the Court of Session Judge, stayed here in 1844, and he described the Hotel as "having the loudest bells and the strongest teethed rats I have ever encountered". After that, he stayed at Aviemore Inn ! The Hotel has been enlarged on several occasions, particularly in 1906, when the new proprietor gave the Hotel its present name. In 1996 there was a disastrous fire and the interior of the Hotel was largely rebuilt.

It is suggested that the walker proceeds up Gynack Road between the Hotel and the Gynack. The public car park behind the Duke of Gordon Hotel was the site of a large distillery called "Speyside". The distillery had been built in 1895, but it only produced whisky until 1905. There is a picture of the old building in the hall of the Duke of Gordon Hotel. The chimney was the first to be demolished and the stone from the chimney and some of the outbuildings was used in the building of the six semi detached villas which overlook the River Gynack, The remaining distillery buildings were demolished in 1925 and that stone was used in the upgrading of the A9. The long row of buildings between the Hotel and the public car park is all that is left of the old distillery, and this row is still known as Distillery Buildings. There is another link with the present. In 1990, a new distillery started production three miles away on the other side of Spey. The whisky was marketed under the name of Drumguish - but it will be seen from the label that it comes from the "Speyside Distillery" founded in 1895.

Where Gynack Road begins to climb, one looks down on the Cross Restaurant. It was built as a tweed mill, later to become a meal mill, then a dwellinghouse, before being practically rebuilt. The explanation for the name is that the cross roads with the traffic lights in the centre of Kingussie was traditionally known as "the Cross"; and when Tony and Ruth Hadley established a small restaurant in a former shop near this junction in 1983, they called their restaurant "The Cross", retaining the name when they restored the old mill and moved their business there in 1997. In conjunction with an earlier generation of mills at the far end of Kingussie, a dam was constructed adjacent to the present restaurant. The Highland Railway took over this dam to provide water for their steam engines. Stone and gravel washed down the Gynack accumulated in the dam and the dam had to be cleared at regular intervals. With the advent of diesel engines, the dam was removed; and this has resulted in the stone and gravel being washed down as far as the station, with flooding in the streets.

Shortly beyond the corner on Gynack Road, a path leads down to a replacement bridge over the river. It might perhaps be mentioned that Robert Louis Stevenson stayed in Kingussie in 1882; and writing much later, he described the Gynack as "the golden burn that pours and sulks in the den behind Kingussie". In an article in the Scots Magazine in 1950, it was stated that older people locally remembered Stevenson most strikingly because he enjoyed sailing paper boats down the Gynack!

Having crossed the bridge, the paths divide. The lower path leads up the wooded glen almost to the Golf Course; and there are way-marked paths beyond, leading to Loch Gynack, and to the summit of Creag Bheag – which towers over Kingussie. Early guide-books relate that on one of the many summits of Creag Beag, there was a cairn in memory of Alexander, the 4th Duke of Gordon (1743 – 1827). There is now no trace of this memorial on Creag Beag, but a fragment of its dedication stone, recording "… by the youths of Kingussie – To the memory of Alx Duke of Gordon – 1828", survives, and it is now carefully preserved in the Folk Museum in Newtonmore.

Until the 19th century, cattle were the principal commodity of the Highlands. The wealth was realised upon the animals being taken overland to the famous public sales or "trysts" at Crieff and latterly at Falkirk, and hence into England. Cattle-raiding was frequent and landowners would commonly pay protection money, or "black mail" for their herds to be protected and for the recovery of stolen cattle. This could be a reputable trade, and indeed in 1658, the Scottish Privy Council authorised the Clan MacGregor to protect the cattle of the Lennox. In a letter to Colonel William Grant of Ballindalloch dated 26 May 1726, Rob Roy MacGregor provided an insight into the cattle rustling which went on at that time. He referred to animals which had belonged to Lachlan Macpherson of Cluny and that he was having a degree of success in identifying particular animals which had been stolen. (As an aside, Rob Roy and Lachlan Macpherson had fought together in the Jacobite Rising of 1715). To counter some of the cattle thieving, "Watches" were set up on strategic hills, and it is significant that Carn an Fhreicadan (the Watch Hill) is located on the skyline behind Kingussie.

Silver and lead ore has been found in the Gynack, but there is no record of any recent mine.

Duke of Gordon Hotel

Kingussie Railway Station

Returning to where the paths divide near the Gynack, we now take the alternative path which leads up to Boa Vista Road. "Boa Vista" is Portuguese for beautiful view, and it is not surprising to learn that Peter Mackenzie (the Count de Serra Largo) built four houses here. At the end of this road, one comes to Ardbroilach Road. This used to be the peat road for the inhabitants of Kingussie, and it was also used as a "short-cut" for those walking over to the River Dulnain and on to Inverness. Further down Ardbroilach Road, and overlooking the whole of Kingussie is the Town Clock. The Clock was erected from funds left by John Duncan McGruer, a native of Kingussie, who emigrated to New Zealand. He had a very successful drapery and importing business in Invercargill; and died in Christchurch in 1923.

Looking over the wall on the right, provides a bird's eye view of St Columba's Churchyard, but it is recommended that the visitor turns right into Mill Road to explore this burial ground. St Columba left Ireland and sailed to Iona with twelve monks in 563 AD; and according to tradition, he established a church here in Kingussie when he was on his way to Inverness. At one time, the churchyard extended down to the River Gynack, but a considerable part of the graveyard was lost when a mill lade was formed, and the road built.

In the mid 1800s the outline of rectangular shape of the old church could still be seen, and in the north gable there was a recess with a piscina or font for the cleaning of consecrated vessels. When the Church of Scotland became divided in 1843, The Kingussie minister and most of his congregation left the Established Church and had no access to the existing church buildings. There is a memory from this time of a minister preaching here from a tent, and the parishioners sitting around on the gravestones.

By the end of the 18th century, the surrounding walls had fallen into disrepair and the whole area was a tangled mess of long grass, rank nettles and dockens. Alexander Macpherson, the banker (and solicitor) in Kingussie, raised funds both in UK and Canada to restore the burial ground. The piscina was eventually found in King Street, having been built into a wall as a copestone. Alexander Macpherson rescued it and it can now be seen - still on a traditional north wall - beneath a tablet which reads

"Here is the hallowed site of the old church of Kingussie, dedicated to St Columba and according to tradition, planted by himself."

The largest plot contains the grave of Col Duncan Macpherson of Breakachy whose wife was a daughter of Cluny of the '45. Behind that plot is the grave of Captain John Macpherson of Ballachroan ("the Black Officer"), who met an untimely end in Gaick in 1800, reputedly at the hands of the Devil. The oldest legible stone is in the middle of the top row – John McPherson, age 5, the son of the Barrackmaster at Ruthven, who died in June 1746 - significantly only a couple of months after the Barracks were destroyed by the Jacobites after the battle of Culloden.

The original flax mill in Kingussie was established in 1799. It was situated at the east end of the town, and water was taken directly from the River Gynack by the mill lade *(An t-Eileach)* which went through St Columba's Churchyard, underneath Ardbroilach Road and then along in a built-in channel at the foot of the steep bank behind the houses of the High Street. This lade was an indispensable institution in the every-day routine of the inhabitants; not only did it drive all the mill wheels, it also supplied almost every household with water. The water was not of the best quality. Latterly, the water was heavily polluted from a carding mill and a waulking mill, and the lade was also a source of dampness. In 1866, the new Town Council being concerned that the mill lade was still the source of domestic water, had the mill lade shut off; and piped water was brought into the town and made accessible by way of "fountains". Significantly, the Ordnance Survey Place Name Book (1868 – 73) under the name "Kingussie" recorded that "The village is well supplied with water lately introduced in pipes from the River Guinach".

Returning along Mill Road and down Ardbroilach Road, one comes to the "Cross" - the crossroads, where it was customary to linger and chat to passers by. Across the High Street is King Street, named after an original merchant in the town – William King. He was better known by the Gaelic translation *An Righ*. Not surprisingly, his son John was appropriately dubbed *Am Prionnsa* - The Prince. Dr Sinton remembered him as a clean-shaven, clean-looking, blue-bonnetted old carl, firm and sedate in his bearing. He died in 1863, aged 86 years.

On the south east corner of the Cross is the Star Hotel. The Ordnance Survey Place Name Book described the original "Star Inn" as a two storey house with good accommodation for travellers. In 1892, William Wolfenden, who was to become provost of Kingussie, built the present building; and high on the gable wall is a plaque bearing Wolfenden's initials. For a short period, the hotel was known as "Wolfenden's Hotel", but when he acquired the Duke of Gordon Hotel, the present name was adopted.

Turning down the High Street, there is the office of the Strathspey Herald. This newspaper, which is published on a Thursday, is the successor to the *Kingussie Record and Badenoch Advertiser* (1902), later to become the *Badenoch Record*. In 1964, the *Badenoch Record* was amalgamated with the Grantown newspaper to become the *Strathspey Herald*.

Beyond the Star Hotel, and recessed from the High Street, is the Court House. Built in 1864 at about the time Kingussie became a burgh, the building has been used as a Sheriff Court and as a Justice of the Peace Court, and for Council meetings; and it is presently being restored – to be used again as public offices.

A short distance beyond the Court House, a close leads to a burial ground *Cladh Meadhon a' Bhaile* ("The Burial-place of the Middle of the Town") which occupies the site of a priory that had been founded by the Earl of Huntly in 1490. At the Reformation in 1560, a plank of bog-fir was fixed into the walls of the church to divide the building. The priest was allowed to officiate in the end which contained the altar, while the Protestant preacher occupied the farther extremity. In 1624, the priory was reconstructed; and the new building became the parish church. However, with the building of a new church in 1792, the stone from the old church was then taken by Captain John Macpherson (the "Black Officer") for the building of a new farm steading at Ballachroan (see chapter 9).

A number of Kingussie proprietors used to keep cattle on common grazings on the other side of the railway. The Chinese restaurant was formerly the house and shop of the shoemaker, James MacIntosh. Jimack, as he was known, kept his cows in a byre behind the shop. Every morning, when I was young, the cows were led down the close and through the town to the common grazings on the other side of the station; the cattle being brought back down the main street in the evening. The routine was particularly memorable as I stayed with an aunt in Tigh an t-Eileach (the "house of the lade"), situated behind Gow's Garage. Jimack's widow, Dorothy Macintosh, continued to run the shoe shop until very recently. Another Kingussie resident who kept cattle was Peter Mackenzie ("Mac") Cumming, sometime

Provost, who had a butchers shop at the Cross, opposite the Star Hotel.

Early in the nineteenth century, when Kingussie was still in its infancy, the Duke of Gordon encouraged a large number of people in various ranks of life to acquire feus (perpetual leases) in the new village at low rates, whereon houses of different sorts and sizes were built according to their means. Some, miscalculating the cost of work and material, were unable to finish in a proper manner dwellings which they had begun. A row of houses near the end of the High Street, was a supreme example. Designed by an ambitious member of the Clan Mackenzie, walls were erected but then for want of funds, the work ceased. For some time, the whole structure remained as a premature ruin until around 1860, it was fitted up in great haste (with outside toilets) to accommodate a horde of navvies engaged in the construction of the railway. Out of jest, the building was given the name "Castle Brahan" - an allusion to the original Castle Brahan which was the family seat of the Seaforths - the Chiefs of the Clan Mackenzie. (That Castle was demolished in 1951).

On the other side of the High Street, set back on a mound, is the Parish Church of Kingussie. This site was known as Tom a' Mhoid. The Wolf of Badenoch used this place as the location for his court; the court being in the centre of the circle of standing stones. (The Wolf of Badenoch was Alastair Mor Mac an Righ, son of King Robert II and great grandson of Robert the Bruce). In 1380, the Wolf of Badenoch summoned the Bishop of Moray to appear before him to settle a dispute over church lands in Badenoch. The Bishop of Moray protested; and when he arrived, he renewed his protest by standing outside the circle of standing stones. For many centuries, the court mound continued to be associated with the administration of justice and the authority of state, but sadly, there is no longer any trace of the standing stones.

The first church on this site was erected in 1792, but it was a considerable time after the church was built before anyone would take up ground for a burial. Indeed, the first to be buried there was a child Catherine Booker, who had taken ill and died at the Inn at Pitmain, where her parents had broken their journey. The grave was built in the shape of a child's cot - a granite wall with iron railings and a marble slab at the head. For many years, this was the only memorial in the churchyard. One of the next to be interred was the minister of the parish, John Robertson, who died in 1825; and eight years

Kingussie Burgh Arms

Three Bridges

later, James Macpherson of Belleville, the only surviving son of James "Ossian" Macpherson (see chapter 3). A prominent gravestone is that of Alexander Macpherson ("the Banker"), sometime Provost of Kingussie; born on 17 February 1839, and died 11 January 1902. There is also a tablet to the memory of the Banker in the Church, and this was replaced after a fire in 1924.

Beyond the Church, one comes to Manse Road where the mill lade went under the main road. Manse Road leads down to what is still called "the Boat House". Before a bridge was built across the Spey at Ruthven, the only means of crossing was either to ford the river further upstream - which was a dangerous exercise - or to take the ferry.

The ferryman was a person of standing in the community, but rather unprincipled. One Communion Sunday, when the Spey was in spate, a large number of folk gathered to be taken across the river. Looking for a quick profit, the ferryman raised his price from one penny to sixpence. Despite pleadings from the churchgoers, he refused to lower his price. They could not afford the fare and so turned back home. But the incident did not go unnoticed. An elder went to the ferryman and cursed him, saying - "For this greed, vengeance will overtake you here and in the hereafter. You will be deprived of your living, your house and your land, and be sure of this: you will die an unnatural death, and your body will be devoured by beasts." This strange prophecy was soon fulfilled. A year later a bridge was built over the Spey and the ferry went out of business. The ferryman worked at odd jobs but never earned enough to keep himself and his family. He finally managed to get work at an old meal mill. One day he was sent to close the mill sluice. To do this he had to walk a narrow plank over a pigsty. When he failed to return the miller went to investigate and found, to his horror, that the ferryman had slipped off the plank and landed among the pigs; the terrified animals then attacked the ferryman and killed him.

The *Scotsman* Newspaper of 27 February 1839 carried a report of a Dr John Macpherson of Kingussie who, having to wait longer than he wished at the ferry, resolved to swim across. The river was in flood, but nevertheless the intrepid Doctor plunged in, having previously placed his watch in the crown of his hat, and then tied the said hat tightly on his head. He was wearing strong boots, and wore a shepherd's plaid; and he was carrying an umbrella. The Doctor, the boots, plaid and umbrella, all landed safe on the opposite side, about a quarter of a mile down the river; and having shaken himself on the bank, the Doctor coolly proceeded, to continue on his way!

Turning into Duke Street, the substantial property at the end of the street has had an interesting history. Prior to 1865, it was occupied by the parish minister, but it was never an ecclesiastical property. Subsequently, it became a shooting lodge, known as Pitmain Lodge. In 1944, the building and the surrounding land was acquired by Dr Isobel Grant, and she established her Highland Folk Museum here.

Running the length of the original Kingussie is Spey Street. Half way along, on the north side is Grianach. "This house, previously known as "Greenfield", is where Robert Louis Stevenson resided between July and September 1882. Confusingly, he referred to the house as "Spey View" and in a letter to his mother dated 30 July he describes it as being "... near my sheltered glen, where I live". While in Kingussie, Stevenson worked on *The Treasure of Franchard*, and he also produced a small book of poems with illustrative woodcuts called *The Graver and the Pen*. At this time, he was printing his own work, using an elementary printing press which can still be seen at the Museum in Lady Stair's House in Edinburgh. His Mother recorded on 14 August – "Fanny (RLS's wife) has been ill since Saturday. We sent for Dr Orchard and he cured her very quickly". That Dr Orchard was the first of three generations of doctor to practice in Kingussie, the last Dr Orchard living and practising at the adjacent house (the "Hermitage").

During his stay in Kingussie, Stevenson arranged a meeting with Ewen Macpherson ("Old Cluny"), the then chief of the Clan. But a change in the weather and a breakdown in his health caused Stevenson to cancel the meeting.

Between 1867 and 1975, Kingussie had the status of a Burgh – with its own Provost and Council. The Council funded the construction of the houses on the corner of Spey Street and King Street; and high up on the King Street elevation, there is a panel of 96 tiles depicting the Arms of the Burgh – unveiled in 1967 to commemorate the centenary of the Burgh.

Alternative walk.

Reference has been made to the bridge over the Gynack where the path divides. The lower path rises gradually through birch woods and come out at Ardbroilach Road. This road leads to Pitmain Estate; and it is a popular walk up this road for about half a mile, then turning left at a signpost "Golf Course Circular". This route drops down to cross the Gynack and then climbs round the top of the Golf Course and then through woodland down to the Golf Course car park. The Leaflet "Kingussie Paths" contains a map showing this route, with the advice to – beware of golf balls !

Chapter 3
Ossian Country

Travelling North from Kingussie, the A9 is elevated with wonderful views over the Spey Meadow and Loch Insh, but it is the old road, the A9152 that is our preferred route. As we shall see, many of the place-names give a clue to the wealth of history in the area.

Shortly after going under the A9, there are a couple of houses on the left of the road. The older house is known as Laggan Cottage – not to be confused with the township and parish of Laggan to the west of Newtonmore. ("Laggan" merely means a "hollow" and the descriptive name also appears elsewhere in Badenoch). In early times, the farm of Laggan was occupied by a famous witch known as *Bean-a-Lagain* or the Wife of Laggan. She was continuously feuding with a neighbouring crofter who complained about her cattle and sheep straying and eating his corn. On one occasion, she reluctantly paid the compensation that he demanded; but shortly after, the crofter's own cattle died and his barn burnt down! Was it a coincidence? Whatever, the crofter had no alternative but to give up his croft and leave the district. His successor was troubled with a black cat raiding his hens.

Eventually he succeeded in wounding the cat in the leg... the cat gave a great scream and disappeared. Next day, the Wife of Laggan was seen walking with a severe limp! Her mischief-making was eventually her downfall. On her final venture, she had taken the form of a hen: this time she was chased by a pack of hounds and torn apart. Her mortal remains were found in her cottage; and her body was taken to the top of the nearby hill and burnt. Looking back, the conical hill on the right of the road *(Tom Cheireag)* is still known locally as the "Witch's Hill". The absence of trees on the hill was attributed to the Witch's curse; but in recent years, scrub trees have grown and the hill is almost obscured from the road. For many years, the hill was the location of the Kingussie War Memorial – now moved to the gardens in front of the Duke of Gordon Hotel; and in place of the War Memorial, there is now a simple stone cairn.

An adjoining house at Laggan has taken the name "Three Bridges". The explanation for this name is to be found after passing the high wall of Kingussie's "New Cemetery". Here the road crosses a small stream which

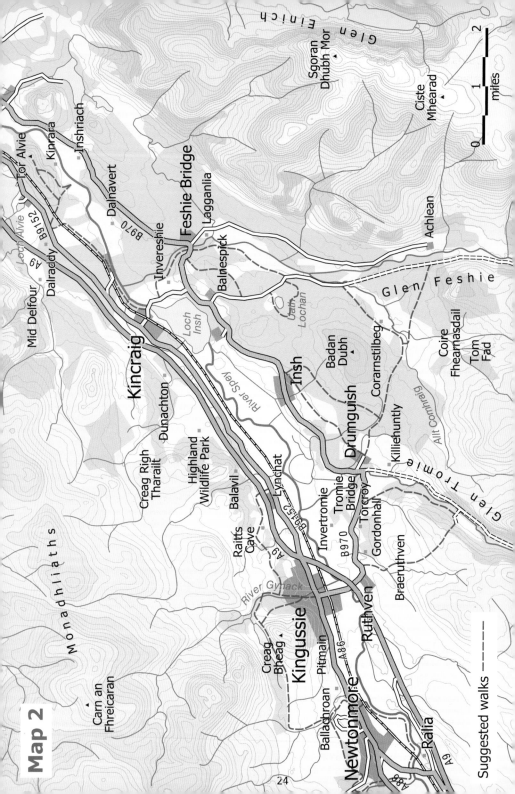

Map 2

Suggested walks ------

24

drains the flood land on the North side of the road. The second bridge is the adjacent railway bridge, and looking under the railway bridge, the reflection of the third bridge can be seen – a single arch, with no parapets... perhaps one of the many bridges built by General Wade when he built his military road from Dunkeld to Inverness in 1728 and 1729. The only practical approach to the old bridge is from the level crossing nearly opposite the New Cemetery; but unfortunately the gates to this crossing are locked. The adjacent structure of three bridges was foreseen by the Brahan Seer *Coinneach Odhar* (Kenneth the Tawny). As well as foreseeing the three bridges, he is said to have predicted the railway. His prophecy was that the road from Perth to Inverness would yet be made so level that an apple could be rolled from the one place to the other.

Of particular note in the near right corner of the New Cemetery, are the graves of nine muslim members of the Royal Indian Army Service Corps who died in and around Glen Feshie during 1942 and 1943 while working with British and Allied servicemen training in Arctic and mountain warfare. They had been brought to the area, ahead of a possible invasion of Norway, and the men had been enlisted to provide mule transportation to support the operation. Several of them drowned after falling into rivers, two took their own lives and the remainder were killed in separate accidents.

Overlooking the flood land is the small village of Lynchat (in Gaelic *Loinn-a-Chait* - the field of the cat). The wild cat still survives in Badenoch, but they are nocturnal and few in number. It was more common in ancient times before it was persecuted, and being the wildest animal known to Highlanders, it was adopted as a symbol by the Clan Macpherson and other clans.

On the hill behind Lynchat is a prehistoric earth house or souterrain (as it is signposted) known locally as Raitts Cave (NH 776 019). ("Raitts" was the old name for the surrounding estate). This cave is to be found by leaving the main road at the end of the village and going through an underpass below the A9, where there is an identified car park. Following the track westwards and parallel to the A9, there is a gate leading into a field. Passing through this gate and walking up the middle of the field, one comes to an enclosure with a small gate leading to *Uaimh Mor*, or "big cave". In 1835, Sir David Brewster, a famous scientist who lived locally, carefully explored the cave. It was then filled with stones and rubbish. On clearing this, he found a long subterranean building, the sides faced with stones, and roofed in gradually by contracting the sides and joining them with large flat stones. Brewster described the lay-out as being like a horse-shoe, having the convex side turned to the south. He added that the entrance was at the middle of the convex side by two stone steps and a long passage. To the left, he found that there was a separate apartment of some length with a door. A lock of unusual form was found among the rubbish. For many years, there was no attempt to protect the site; and the approach to the "cave" has deteriorated significantly.

In the 14th century, there was intense rivalry between the Clan Macpherson and the Clan Macniven - who also lived in Badenoch. The disputes frequently involved the ownership of cattle. Relations deteriorated, the Macnivens insulted the Macphersons and the feud came to a climax. One night, over a hundred Macphersons surprised the Macnivens, and only eighteen survived. They found refuge in the woods around Raitts, and it is said that they constructed this cave under the floor of a farmhouse. One of the Macphersons became suspicious that there was a hiding place in this house. He dressed himself as a beggar and came to the house late one evening. The women of the house took pity on him, and when he feigned illness, they allowed him to stay overnight. During the night, the women employed themselves baking oatcakes. As soon as these were ready they were placed in the bottom of a cupboard and instantly disappeared. Suspecting that the fugitives were concealed in a cave below the house, the "beggar" left the house at an early hour; and returned some days later with a strong party, and that ended the remaining Macnivens. During the eighteenth century the cave was also the haunt of a gang of robbers.

Traces of about 500 souterrain have been found in Scotland, dating back to the later iron age (300 BC to 300 AD). The purpose of these constructions is not known, but they may have been used for the storage of dairy products. A recently discovered souterrain in excellent condition, can be found at Kilvaxter, some miles north of Uig, in Skye.

A few hundred yards above Raitts Cave, in the same field, are the ruins of the ancient township of Easter Raitts which was "cleared" of its inhabitants early in the 19th century. Between 1996 and 2000, these ruins were extensively excavated by archeologists and fully documented, some of the finds dating back to the neolithic age. The results of the excavations have since been

Raitts Cave

Raitts Cave

used to form the basis for the "Township" in the Highland Folk Museum at Newtonmore.

The farm adjacent to Lynchat is known as Chapelpark, The name in Gaelic signifies *Pairc-an-t-Seipell*, derived from a chapel and churchyard that once were there, and known as the Chapel of McLuac, an Irish saint who may have been an associate of St Columba. At one time, the place was called "Tillie-Sow", the name being corrupted from the Gaelic – there having been an inn at this location, whose entrance door was surmounted by the motto *Tadhailibh so* ("Visit here" or "Stay here").

Two or three hundred yards further on, topping a knoll to the left, is an object that is surrounded by many interesting associations; but which, being almost obscured by intervening trees, is likely to escape the observation of the casual passer-by. This is a handsome marble obelisk, erected to the memory of James Macpherson, the most famous native of Badenoch. Such was his vanity that he himself bequeathed £500 in his will for the erection of this memorial! James Macpherson was born at Invertromie in 1736, his father being Andrew Macpherson, the brother of Lachlan of Nuide, who became chief of Clan Macpherson. One of James' boyhood recollections was of throwing stones at the government troops burning down Ruthven Barracks in 1746. He was educated at the Grammar School of Inverness, and at the Universities of Aberdeen and Edinburgh. This was followed by teaching in the village of Ruthven (now no more!), and in private tutoring. He became an enthusiast in the study of old Highland literature, and travelled all over the Highlands, collecting what he believed to be the genuine remains of the great Ossianic poetry of the Highlands. This was a time when extensive Gaelic verse had come down, through generation after generation, without even having been committed to paper. In 1760, he published what he stated to be a translation of some fragments of this ancient poetry; and in 1761, he published *Fingal; an ancient Epic Poem in Six Books, with several other Poems, composed by Ossian, the son of Fingal, translated from the Gaelic Language*. Shortly after, *Temora* was published. *Fingal* and *Temora* were epic poems in the same form as Homer's *Iliad* and *Odyssey* and Virgil's *Aeneid*. It is never suggested that Homer and Virgil did other than collate many traditional legends and set them down in verse. James Macpherson followed in the same tradition, except that his source material was in Gaelic and he presented his material in English. Perhaps he was wrong to use the word "translated" in his title. It was this that Dr Johnson seized upon and implied that the whole material was a work of fiction. To this day the question of the authorship of the poems is not authoritatively settled. If James Macpherson did improve and add to some of the poems that he collected, he was so fully into the spirit of the age that he was able to write verse remarkably similar to the fragments which were admittedly genuine.

Meanwhile, James Macpherson was advancing himself in public life. He became the agent in London for Mohammad Ali Khan Wallajah, the Nawab (or Nabob) of Arcot, who was at that time an ally of the British India Company and the effective ruler of much of South India. This brought him great wealth, and in 1780, James Macpherson purchased a seat in the British Parliament at a cost of £5,000, supposedly as representative for the Cornish borough of Camelford. James Macpherson died in 1796. Up to the end of his life, his parliamentary duties and the business of the Nawab compelled him to spend most of the year in London; and it was only during a few months in the summer and autumn that he was able to enjoy his property in the Highlands. He never married, but in his will, he made provision for each of his five children.

Surrounding the Memorial is a burial ground for the Brewster Macphersons, descendants of James Macpherson. Also in the burial ground is a propeller blade from an Avro Lancaster bomber, commemorating the loss of six Australian and one British crewmen when a Lancaster exploded in mid-air at about 10,000 feet on 31 August 1944. Debris that was scattered over two square miles of adjacent country, was recovered between 2008 and 2010 and it was then that the memorial was erected.

The ancient Castle of Raitts was at one time the principal stronghold of the Cummings (Comyns). Their chief, jealous of the neighbouring Laird of Mackintosh, invited him and his kindred to a great banquet for the atrocious purpose of slaughtering his guests unawares. The company were to be so arranged at table in such a way that the Mackintoshes would be separated from one another, and the appearance of a boar's head was to be the signal for each Cumming to stab the stranger who sat beside him. Mackintosh discovered the plot. Nevertheless, he accepted the invitation, having previously informed his clansmen of the signal, and warned them to anticipate their treacherous entertainers. Accordingly, when the boar's head was introduced, the Mackintoshes seized the moment, and with the barbarity common in those dark and bloody days, they inflicted the most ample and speedy revenge on their foes. Thus the estate of Raitts came to be Mackintosh country. However, the Mackintosh of Borlum family, which owned Raitts, had an unfortunate history. It is said that Edward Mackintosh, the last resident Borlum, murdered one of his servants for refusing to go along with him across the Spey to rob the house of a weaver in Killiehuntly where it was known that there was a great deal of money. Eventually, in 1770, Borlum attempted unsuccessfully to rob Sir Hector Monro of Novar* (1727-1806), on his journey north after his return from India. Borlum fled to America; but three of his accomplices, one of them his own brother, were seized and hanged at Inverness.

Edward Mackintosh's wife was a sister of Colonel Duncan Macpherson of Breakachy, and she remained on the Estate after her husband's departure. Mrs Mackintosh, although in straitened circumstances, continued to display the style and manners of an old Highland lady. It is related that on one occasion after dining at Kinrara with the Duchess of Gordon, some gentlemen insisted upon accompanying her to the door to see her into her carriage. Her protestations were to no avail; and the reason for her reluctance became apparent when, much to the amusement of the onlookers, Lady Borlum climbed into a common farm cart, which was awaiting her, took her seat on a bale of straw, and so departed.

In 1788, James Macpherson succeeded in buying the Estate. He commissioned Robert Adam to design a substantial mansion on the site of the original Raitts Castle. The new house, completed in 1790, was named Belleville – the French for "beautiful town". The site of the house had previously been known to Gaelic-speaking people as *Bail-a-bhile* – the town on the brae-top; and it is perhaps appropriate that the house is now known as Balavil. Elizabeth Grant of Rothiemurchus, in her Memoirs of a Highland Lady described the house as "a great hospital-looking place." A fire in 1903, largely destroyed the house, but it was rebuilt; and it can easily be seen from the road.

Proceeding north, one comes to the Highland Wildlife Park, in extensive grounds on the shoulder of the hill. Originally set up in 1972 for native animals, it has since been taken over by the Royal Zoological Society of Scotland, and now has a range of animals representing every part of the world. Of Highland interest is a number of wildcat, this exhibit having being sponsored by the Clan Macpherson Association since 1992.

The next mansion, which is not visible from the road, is Dunachton, at one time the Badenoch residence of the Mackintosh of Mackintosh, the chief of the Clan Mackintosh. Dunachton in Gaelic is *Dun-Neachdainn*, the hill fort of Nechtan. According to tradition, Nechtan was a Pictish king; and some speculate that it was here that the battle of Nechtansmere was fought in 685 AD between the Picts and the Angles. Close to the Dunachton Burn, there is a ridge with the name *Creag Righ Tharailt* (King Harold's rock), suggesting that Norsemen, perhaps in the 9th century, penetrated this far inland. There is a tradition that a leader of these invaders died in battle and was buried on this hillside.

In 1870, on the demolishing of an old steading, a Pictish stone was discovered. This stone, which had the rough carving of an animal, has since been erected on a sandstone base in the walled garden adjacent to the House.

In 1924, Dr Isobel Grant, the founder of Am Fasgach, which is now the Folk Museum at Newtonmore, wrote *Everyday life on an Old Highland Farm*, based on the records kept by her ancestor William Mackintosh, who farmed at Dunachton in the latter part of the 18th century. A century later, the grandparents of George T Hay were tenant farmers at Dunachton, and in his *Perth and North Thereof* (1966), he vividly describes the life of this Highland community.

In a corner of Dunachton Estate, near to the road, there is an ancient churchyard which at one time contained the ruins of a chapel dedicated to St Drostan, another of the many Celtic saints associated with St Columba.

Beyond the chapel, the road takes us to Kincraig.

* The same Hector Munro, who as a young Ensign, pursued Cluny of the '45.

Suggested walk

A scenic walk is to combine the "Tom Baraidh Circular" and "Raitts township" routes, which are featured in the "Kingussie Paths" leaflet. From the traffic lights in Kingussie, Ardbroilach Road leads upwards to the Pitmain Estate road. About a 1/4 mile beyond the Estate gate, a signpost leads into the Tom Baraidh wood. Keeping to the left, the path leads to a sign for "Raitts". The path is now in open country and gradually climbs on to the moor with panoramic views over the Spey valley. Below the viewpoint, the path goes through what remains of the township and then passes the fenced enclosure containing Raitts Cave. Below this enclosure, a track leads to Chaplepark Farm and Lynchat, from where a service bus can take you back to Kingussie.

Chapter 4

Alvie

The lands to the north east of Kincraig are dominated by the Estates of Alvie and Kinrara. Leaving Kincraig, our route takes us in a northerly direction along the B9152, passing Alvie school on the left and the former Free Church (now a dwelling house) on the right.

Within Alvie Estate is an ancient relic of Druidical times, perhaps dating to 2000 BC. Following the signposts for Alvie Stables, one comes to a paddock opposite Mid Delfour. Immediately beyond the paddock, there is an impressive standing stone, about nine feet high, and adjacent to this stone are two concentric circles of about 25 feet and 55 feet in diameter (NH 844 086). The standing stone and another large stone now lying horizontally, may have signified the entrance to this sacred site. There is no record of any serious excavation. Were the stones associated with some ancient rite? - we shall never know. On leaving this site, it is possible to continue on the same estate road, but this takes you on to the A9, with little opportunity for further exploring. It is therefore recommended that the same route is followed back to the B9152.

Continuing in a northerly direction, a track on the left at a "50 mph" sign, leads to Dalraddy, at one time the lands of the Macphersons of that name. On the other side of the B9152 is the Dalraddy Holiday Park, and on the left of that entrance, a road leads into Kinrara Estate. The history of Kinrara is closely associated with Alexander, 4th Duke of Gordon, his wife Jane, and their son George, the 5th and last Duke of Gordon.

Tor Alvie, with a tall column on its summit, is a prominent landmark over much of Badenoch. There are no signposts, but if one follows the estate road over the railway and takes a track to the left, you come upon a large open field. At the top of this field, there is a gate from which a track leads gradually upwards among a juniper woodland. A few yards to the right of the track, one may find the Waterloo Cairn. This cairn is of particular interest because there are very few war memorials erected prior to the Boer War. Prior to the 5th Duke of Gordon inheriting the title from his father, George was known as the Marquis of Huntly. Two of his personal friends had been killed at Waterloo and George took a sudden fancy to build a cairn in their honour on this site. George drove forward the construction with such fury that it was completed only a few weeks after the battle. He clearly intended that the cairn should not be a source of sadness. It is said that behind the copper door that bears the inscription, there is a miniature wine-cellar which was intended to provide refreshment for his shooting-parties. The memorial was unveiled on August 16 of that year by George himself before a gathering of nobility and landed gentry who then dined convivially with him at his hunting-seat of Kinrara, below. Alexander Macpherson, the Banker in Kingussie (writing in 1893) observed that "the strong copper door remains as securely fastened as the door of a famous wine-cellar in Edinburgh belonging to a well-known total abstainer". The door is as secure as ever, as there is still no trace of the key.

The inscription on the door reads as follows -

TO THE MEMORY OF
SIR ROBERT MACARA
OF THE 42D REGIMENT, OR ROYAL HIGHLANDERS;
COLONEL JOHN CAMERON
OF THE 92D REGIMENT, OR GORDON HIGHLANDERS
AND THEIR BRAVE COUNTRYMEN
WHO GLORIOUSLY FELL AT THE BATTLE OF WATERLOO IN JUNE 1815.

Erected by The Most Noble the MARQUIS OF HUNTLY, August 16th, 1815

The 42nd Regiment is now better known as the Black Watch. Robert Macara was the Colonel of the Regiment at the time, but strangely his rank does not appear on the inscription. The inscription implies that Macara and Cameron were killed at Waterloo, but in fact, they were both killed in a skirmish at Quatre Bas, two days before the famous battle. Cameron was a brother-in-law of Duncan Macpherson of Cluny (Duncan of the Kiln), the son of Cluny of the '45. It is also interesting to note that the reference to the "brave countrymen" who also fell, appears to have been added as an afterthought.

Continuing on the Tor Alvie path, one finally reaches the base of the Column. The inscription tells us, in English, Gaelic and Latin, that it was erected

Mid Delfour - Standing Stone

Stone Circle

IN MEMORY OF

HIS GRACE GEORGE, FIFTH AND LAST DUKE OF GORDON, G.C.B.,

GENERAL IN THE BRITISH ARMY,
COLONEL OF THE THIRD REGIMENT OF FOOT GUARDS,
GOVERNOR OF THE CASTLE OF EDINBURGH,
LORD LIEUTENANT OF ABERDEENSHIRE, ETC. ETC. ETC.,
WHO DIED ON THE 28TH OF MAY 1836,
IN THE SIXTY-SIXTH YEAR OF HIS AGE

He was a generous Landlord, a patriotic Highlander, and a brave Soldier - at once the delight of the Noble and the Friend of the Poor.

Ewen Macpherson ("Old Cluny") - son of Duncan of the Kiln - played a major part in having the monument erected; and the name of Ewen Macpherson, and the names of the other sponsors, are recorded on the fourth side of the Column.

George, the 5th and last Duke of Gordon, was born in 1770. His father (Alexander, the 4th Duke) had raised the 92nd Regiment, the Gordon Highlanders; and at the age of 25, George, then known as the Marquis of Huntly, commanded the regiment in the early stages of the Napoleonic wars. However, this was the time of big spending, such as ruined many Highland estates. George, was in financial difficulties from an early age. Indeed, a contemporary described Lord Huntly as being "in the decline of his rackety life, overwhelmed with debts, sated with pleasure and tired of fashion". His marriage into a wealthy family eased some of his problems, but his indebtedness continued until he succeeded to the Gordon Estates on the death of his father in 1827. An American journalist, gave an interesting account of life at Gordon Castle in the twilight years of the 5th Duke's life, describing a "rich private world peopled by ladies cantering sidesaddle on palfreys, ladies driving nowhere in particular in phaetons, gentlemen with guns, keepers with hounds and terrier at heel, and everywhere a profusion of fallow deer, hares and pheasants." Not surprisingly, much of the Gordon Estates in Badenoch had to be sold after George's death.

George's father (Alexander, the 4th Duke of Gordon), also had a tempestuous lifestyle. In 1767 he married the 19 year old Jane Maxwell. From the start, neither she nor the Duke made any particular effort to be faithful to the other. Latterly, the Duke lived in retirement at Gordon Castle, near Fochabers. Such was his disreputable lifestyle that he was the father to four children born to a Jane Christie, and indeed the Duke married her after the Duchess died. In contrast, Jane Maxwell was in the centre of society. She was a celebrated beauty, and is best remembered for placing the King's shilling between her teeth to help recruitment to the Gordon Highlanders. The land at Kinrara was given over to Jane as part of a settlement against her unfaithful husband; and she designed and built Kinrara House which lies on the south side of Tor Alvie overlooking the Spey.

Some distance to the west of Kinrara House is an enclosed water source known as St Eata's Well. Little is known of St Eata. He was a native of Northumbria and as a boy, he was taken to the Holy Island of Lindisfarne where he was trained as a monk. At that time, Lindisfarne was one of the centres of the Celtic Church, and the community there worshipped out of doors around high standing crosses - surrounded by the earth, the sea and the sky. In 651 Eata was elected Abbot of Melrose – the only known Scottish connection. In the year 664, the Celtic Church and the Roman Church came together, and Eata adopted the Roman customs. Eata became a bishop in 678 and was latterly Bishop of Hexham where he died in 686. A chapel near the Spey was also dedicated to St Eata. Prior to 1812 the site was quite visible but there is now no trace.

However, in a secluded corner overlooking the Spey, there can still be found the monument dedicated to the memory of Jane, the celebrated Duchess of Gordon, who died in 1812. It is said that the monument was erected on the site of St Eta's chapel. Jane possessed a capacity for match-making which was unrivaled. Of her five daughters, three were married to Dukes, (Richmond, Manchester and Bedford) and one to a Marquess (Cornwallis). Each of those daughters, their respective husbands, and their children are all named on this Memorial; but strangely, there is no reference to George, her eldest son, whose monument is on the top of Tor Alvie. It might perhaps be mentioned that when Jane's second daughter Louisa, was about to marry (later to become the 2nd Marquess Cornwallis), there was hesitation on account of some supposed insanity in the Gordon family. Jane resolved this by giving the gratifying assurance that there was not a drop of Gordon blood in Louisa!

Returning to the B 9152, and proceeding northwards, takes us to Alvie Church, which is set on a raised promontory overlooking Loch Alvie. William Gordon, was the minister at the time of the 1745 Rising. He attempted to remain strictly neutral. However, many of the Highlanders were reduced to privation after Culloden and were hospitably received at his manse. The news of this reached the ears of the Duke of Cumberland, and Mr Gordon was summoned to appear before the Duke and required to answer for himself. It is said that he addressed Cumberland as follows:

"May it please your Royal Highness, I am exceedingly straitened between two contrary commands, both coming from very high authority.

My heavenly King's Son commands me to feed the hungry, to clothe the naked, to give heat and drink to my very enemies, and to relieve, to the very utmost of my power indiscriminately all objects of distress that come in my way.

My earthly King's son (the Duke of Cumberland himself) commands me to drive the homeless wanderer from my door, to shut my bowels of compassion against the cries of the needy, and to withhold from my fellow-mortals in distress the relief which it is in my power to afford.

Pray which of these commands am I to obey?"

It is said that the Duke of Cumberland was so impressed with the humane feelings and noble sentiments of the worthy minister, that he felt constrained to reply: "By all means obey the commands of your heavenly King's Son".

Passing reference might be made to the use of whisky at funerals in the Highlands. Too often, this turned into abuse. People often came long distances on foot to funerals, and the body had frequently to be carried over many miles. On one occasion, the Minister at Alvie was kept waiting in the churchyard for such a funeral. Two hours after the stipulated time, he set out to meet the funeral, which was coming from the west end of the parish. On reaching the Moor of Alvie, about a mile and a half from the church, he found the body lying at the side of the road - and the whole of the funeral company already inebriated and engaged in a free fight. Boldly he stepped in and attempted to separate them. Among the party was a well-known bully, who made a rush at the minister and attempted to trip him. The minister, however, seized his antagonist and threw him with such force to the ground that he lay unconscious for some minutes. This incident brought all the mourners to their senses, and the body was then lifted up and carried in silence to the churchyard. On this occasion, the minister further punished the company by ordering them away as soon as the grave was closed, without allowing them to partake of the customary refreshments in the churchyard.

Alvie Church was built in 1798. When it was renovated in 1880, the bones of 150 skeletons were found under the floor. The circumstances may never be known. However, there may be a clue in James Thomson's *Recollections of a Speyside Parish* (1888) where the author describes a gravedigger at the bottom of a deep grave at the old Kirk of Aberlour, taking out a very large skull, and observes -

"I have never been able to account for the repulsive practice, common in my boyish days, of lifting the decaying bones of the dead from the grave when a new internment was made in it. One of the most remarkable sights that I have seen is the so-called "Ripon bonehouse." The vaults below the Cathedral are filled with bones that have been disinterred from the surrounding graveyard. They are piled away pretty much like wine bottles in a cellar."

Beyond Alvie, the road leaves Badenoch, and so we return to Kincraig.

Suggested Walk

An alternative walk might begin by taking the service bus to Dalraddy Holiday Park, and following the Speyside Way from there back to Kincraig. Follow the road towards the caravan site and after a short distance, take a track to the left which leads under the railway, meeting the Speyside Way at this point.

Celtic Bell in Insh Church

Chapter 5

Through Kincraig

Opposite the war memorial at Kincraig, there is a Celtic cross in the garden of the Church Hall. The inscription, which is now heavily weathered, reads

> This cross has been
> erected in memory of
> Piper Peter Stewart
> and his brave comrades
> who for Queen and country
> fell in the battle of Atbara
> on the Nile on April VIII
> MDCCCXCVIII (1898)

It is said that this is the only known memorial to a single piper. Prior to this time, most of the surrounding community were adherents of the Free Church. Men who had enlisted in the army were regarded as "rolling stones" and were condemned from the pulpit. Towards the end of the 19th century, the minister of the established Church brought many parishioners back to his church. He raised the necessary funds to commemorate this local man; and there was a strong military presence for the unveiling of the monument. However, the events were somewhat marred by the news that over the day, the recruiting sergeant had persuaded seven local men to enlist!

Turning into the village of Kincraig, we pass the entrance to the former station. Within two months of the completion of the station in 1863, a new shop was opened in a wooden hut. Such was the increased trade that five years later, the shop moved into a purpose built general store. At that time, the range of its merchandise included the revolutionary new paraffin lamps and a full range of clothing including bowler hats, white collars and made-up black ties - especially for funerals. A shop in Kincraig continues to serve the local community, but with a greatly reduced range of wares.

Prior to the building of the present wooden bridge over the Spey in 1874, there was a ford and a ferry boat, and the location was known as Boat of Insh - "Insh" being the parish which extended South and East from the Spey, between the River Feshie and the River Tromie. When the railway opened in

1863, the station was appropriately named "Boat of Insh."; but there was already an Insch Station on the line between Aberdeen and Inverness, and the confusion caused the Railway Company to looked around, and the name of the local farm of Kincraig was adopted for the station. The new community which was built around the station, came to be known as "Kincraig Station", and now simply "Kincraig". (There was a similar problem with the community of Abernethy - south of Grantown-on Spey. A station named "Abernethy" already existed in Fife; and in that case, the new station was called Nethy Bridge).

On an afternoon in September 1860, the ferryman encountered a party of ladies and gentlemen who wished to be taken over the Spey. They were duly ferried across in the "big boat"; and on landing one of the gentlemen inquired how much there was to pay. This would at most have been a shilling or two, but into the ferryman's hand was placed two golden guineas. With a smile and a "good-day", the generous strangers disappeared, leaving the ferryman to congratulate himself upon his good fortune and to wonder who the party could be. In due course it leaked out that they had been Queen Victoria and Prince Albert, with a few attendants, travelling incognito. This information brought scorn upon the ferryman, however, as it was recalled that he had kept on his bonnet in Her Majesty's presence.

In her Journal, the Queen vividly describes her experience -

"...we came upon Loch Insh, which is lovely, and of which I should have liked exceedingly to have taken a sketch. The light was lovely; and some cattle were crossing a narrow strip of grass across the end of the loch nearest us, which really made a charming picture. It is not a wild lake, quite the contrary; no high rocks, but woods and blue hills as a background... at the ferry, we parted from the ponies, only Grant and Brown coming on with us. Walker, the police inspector, met us, but did not keep with us. He had been sent to order everything in a quiet way, without letting people suspect who we were: in this he entirely succeeded. The ferry was a very rude affair; it was like a boat or cobble, but we could only stand upon it, and it was moved at one end by two long oars, plied by the ferryman and Brown, and at the other end by a long sort of beam which Grant took in hand. A few seconds brought us over to the road, where there were two shabby vehicles... each with a pair of small and rather miserable horses."

The River Feshie joins the Spey about a mile downstream from Kincraig. In Glen Feshie, many acres of what was at one time arable land have been washed away. Every big flood deposits stones and gravel, and as a result, the lower reaches of the river are characterised on either side by an immense expanse of *claddagh* (literally a "beach"). These stones are finally deposited at the confluence of the Spey and the Feshie, in the form of a large gravel bank, thereby increasing the level of Loch Insh and the water table of the meadows upstream of the Loch. Early in 1901 the level of the road leading from the bridge was raised; but in times of great flood, the road can still be covered by water, as there is a reluctance to clear the gravel spit at the mouth of the Feshie.

The osprey, a fish eagle, was absent from the Scottish scene in the first half of the 20th century. They returned to breed at Loch Garten in about 1953, and there are now more than 100 breeding pairs throughout the Highlands. They migrate to West Africa at the end of August each year, returning the following April. Pairs of birds use the same nest site every year. Looking west from the bridge at Kincraig, an osprey nest can be seen high up on the wooded island, and in the Summer, it is usually possible to see these wonderful birds, either at the nest or fishing over Loch Insh.

A short distance from the bridge, at the side of the Loch, there is a gate and a path climbing steeply up to Insh Church. The church is always open. The church was linked to the family of Macpherson of Invereshie. The present building dates from 1792 with renovations in 1912 (when the cobbled floor was removed) and 1963. The engraved cross in the north east window dates from this latter time. However, the site of the church has reputedly been a place of Christian worship since the 6th century, and the earliest church was dedicated to St Adamnan (625 -704), a disciple of St Columba. The mound on which the church stands is known as Tom Eunan ("Eunan" is a diminutive of Adamnan).

In an alcove that used to be the original entrance and vestry to the building, hangs a very old bell. This ancient bronze bell was made in about 900 AD, and is one of only five such bells remaining in Scotland. It may have been used by the Culdees, as the monks were then known, to call people to worship. The bell is associated with St Adamnan causing some to believe that it is much older. According to tradition, the bell was once carried away south by a party of marauders. Evidently grieving over its removal, the bell never could be silenced, but continued to cry "Tom Eunan", "Tom Eunan". In some unexplained way it escaped from the thieves, and its calls were so vigorous that the neighbourhood was aroused: the bell was welcomed home, taken into the Church and foreverafter chained.

Where are these other bells? The best known is the St Fillans bell which was used in the coronation of King James IV at Scone on 24 June 1488. A legend associated with this bell is that it was placed over a sufferer's head during healing rituals in order to cure such afflictions as migraine headaches. This bell also had the reputation of flying back on its own accord. However, one day a visitor who was unaccustomed to seeing bells flying through the air, was startled and shot it with an arrow, causing a crack. This bell is now on permanent display in the Royal Scottish Museum in Chamber Street, Edinburgh.

Less accessible is the bell on St Finnan's Isle in Loch Sheil in Moidart. St Finnan followed in the footsteps of Saint Columba from Iona, living on the island and spreading the Christian faith as far as Lochaber. The tradition was continued by other missionaries from Iona for many centuries after his death. On the island (also known as the Green Isle), there are the remains of an old church, ruined since the 1700s. The church was thought to have been a simple, stoned-roofed building with a crudely crafted altar and this bell can still be found on the altar stone. The bell is reputedly bewitched, and that anyone removing it soon becomes distressed. On one occasion, a platoon of troops returning to Fort William removed the bell; but on reaching Glenfinnan the local clansmen apprehended the soldiers, tied them to trees and thrashed them. Whenever the bell has been taken it has always returned, flying back on its own or carried on the back of a swan. The island is also an ancient burial place and still contains many ancient crosses. Moidart is still a traditionally Catholic district. The Catholic graves are all on the north side of the island, and the Presbyterian graves are on the south side. There is no ferry, and no boats for hire so the island is practically inaccessible. Forteviot Church in Perthshire also has a similar bell.

The remaining bell was to be found at Little Dunkeld. It is believed that this bell may have been cast for King Malcolm III (Malcolm Canmore), at the time the relics of St Columba were brought to Dunkeld - the geographical centre of his newly enlarged kingdom. With a prominent Cathedral in the area, the question is asked why such a relic is linked to Little Dunkeld Kirk and not

Dunkeld Cathedral. The answer may lie in the time when Rome re-asserted its authority over the Celtic Church in places like Scotland. The Cathedral was the centre of the new Roman form of church and therefore relics of the former Celtic church were not welcome. An ancient story tells of robbers who stole the bell and headed off into the hills with their plunder. When they stopped for a rest they placed the bell on a rock. They could not move the bell until they turned to face Dunkeld once more with the intention to return it. The Dunkeld bell is not on display, but a replica can be seen in the Cathedral.

Leaving Insh Church, a short distance along the road takes us to the white gateposts and the avenue leading to Invereshie House. The house is privately owned, but there is an attractive right of way to the left of the gateway, which takes walkers to Feshie Bridge.

By tradition, the Clan Macpherson was represented by three main lineages, the Macphersons of Cluny, the Macphersons of Pitmain and the Macphersons of Invereshie. Invereshie is the most northerly part of the Clan country, and is formed by a triangle with the River Spey on the north west and the River Feshie on the east.

In 1637, the Gordon family sold the lands of Dalraddy to Paul Macpherson, younger of Dalraddy. In the same year Angus Macpherson of Invereshie, acquired all the land between the rivers Feshie and Tromie. Towards the end of the 17th century, the then Invereshie family got into financial difficulties. The grandson of Paul was the purchaser, and the whole lands of Dalraddy and Invereshie were conjoined. Across the Feshie was Mackintosh land, and in 1661 the two clans nearly came to armed conflict over the Mackintosh's attempt to erect a mill on the river. This would have interfered with a Macpherson mill downstream. The feiry cross went out and the Macphersons rallied in strength. Mackintosh, finding himself outnumbered, appealed to other clans in the area, including the Grants; but there was a longstanding friendship between the Macphersons and the Grants, and they refused to become involved. In 1806, George Macpherson of Invereshie succeeded as heir to General Grant of Ballindalloch and adopted the name "Macpherson Grant". Following on the death of the 4th Duke of Gordon in 1827, Sir George Macpherson Grant, as he became known, acquired the Estates of Alvie, on the other side of the Spey, and Invertromie in the south, extending his lands to the borders of Aberdeenshire and Perthshire.

Insh Church

Feshie Bridge

Invereshie House has its origins in 1685, but the major part of the house was built by Sir George Macpherson Grant in 1830. It was Sir George who leased upper Glen Feshie – to become known as Glenfeshie Estate – to the Duke and Duchess of Bedford. Georgina, the Duchess, was the youngest daughter of the 4th Duke of Gordon. Georgina promoted the sporting potential of the estate; but she is best known for her friendship with the famous painter, Sir Edward Landseer, and many of his famous paintings of the red deer are from this period. On the death of Sir George Macpherson Grant, the 5th Baronet, in 1951, Invereshie Estate was divided and sold; and the interests of the Macpherson Grant family are now centred on Ballindalloch.

This is perhaps the appropriate stage to relate the story of James Macpherson, born to an Invereshie Macpherson and a beautiful gipsy in 1675. It is said that his father was killed shortly after the birth while pursuing a body of hostile clansmen who had been cattle-lifting. Notwithstanding, the Invereshie family continued to acknowledge the relationship, and supported mother and child. James grew up to be a man "magnificent in stature and intellect and possessing beauty, strength and stature rarely equalled". He was also an excellent fiddler (violinist) – of which more will follow. Sadly, James followed his mother into the life of a gipsy, conducting himself as a freebooter and pillaging property throughout the North East of Scotland.

James Macpherson escaped several times from his captors. In Aberdeen, he was rescued from prison by his cousin, Donald Macpherson and a gipsy named Peter Brown, aided by the populace. Shortly afterwards, he was captured by Duff of Braco, after a woman dropped a blanket over him from a window, and he was disarmed before he could get free of it. He was rescued by the Lord of Grant, who was in opposition to Duff's methods of administration, but on the same evening, he was again captured, along with three of his party, Peter Brown, James Gordon and Donald Brown; and all were immediately removed to Banff prison by Duff, under strong escort. The four prisoners were brought to trial and James Macpherson was sentenced to death at a public hanging on 16 November 1700.

The local inhabitants raised a petition for his reprieve. On the day of the execution, Duff saw a lone rider coming from Turriff and correctly assumed that he carried a pardon from Lord Grant. Duff then set about turning the town clock 15 minutes ahead and so James Macpherson was hanged before the pardon arrived. The magistrates allegedly were punished for this and the town clock was kept 15 minutes ahead of the correct time for many years.

While awaiting execution, James composed a song and air beginning -

> I've spent my life in rioting,
> Debauch'd my health and strength,
> I squander'd fast, as pillage came,
> And fell to shame at length.

Legend has it that before he was hanged, he treated the crowd to a rendering of this tune and then offered his fiddle to anyone who would play it at his wake. When no one came forward to take the fiddle, he broke it across his knee and threw it into the crowd with the remark, "No one else shall play Jamie Macpherson's fiddle". A cousin picked up the pieces; they found their way to Cluny Castle, and the remains of the fiddle are now in the Clan Macpherson Museum in Newtonmore.

The Banff clock was removed from its tower in 1796, and acquired by James Duff the 4th Earl of Fife, so that he could build it into his new Clock Tower at the hamlet of Balvenie, which became known as Dufftoun (Dufftown) after him. Around 1965, the mechanism was electrified, and the clock is now also in the Macpherson Museum along with a replica of James' two-handed sword, the original having been lost in Duff House.

The father of Robert Burns, the poet, was of North East farming stock. He left his native Mearns, now a part of south Aberdeenshire, to find work and eventually settle in Ayrshire. On his northern tour, Burns visited Banff in 1787; and he wrote his song "Macpherson's Farewell" as a consequence of what he heard from the Banff locals of the celebrated freebooter.

> Sae rantingly, sae wantonly
> Sae dauntingly gaed he
> He play'd a spring and danc'd it round
> Below the gallows tree.

Beyond Invereshie, the Outdoor Centre at Loch Insh is a reminder of a more recent battle. There were early records of rafting small quantities of timber down the River Spey to Garmouth. In 1730 the York Building Company bought woods in Abernethy, and commenced operations on an extensive scale. Proper rafts were constructed, and with the improved methods of transporting the timber to the sea, the trade increased in magnitude; and was only superseded upon the opening of the Highland Railway in 1863.

The late Clive Freshwater established his Outdoor Centre at Loch Insh in 1969 and shortly after, he was served with a writ by an Estate claiming that canoeists could damage salmon fishing on the River Spey. The battle went on for four years. Eventually the House of Lords accepted the evidence of the rafting and confirmed the public right of navigation on the River Spey. Significantly the "right to roam" legislation enacted in 2003 now includes a right of access to navigable waters.

Suggested walk

Reference has already been made to a right of way. This begins at Feshie Bridge and passes the Forestry Commission car park and the Frank Bruce sculptures (see the next chapter). Thereafter, the path goes through the wood between Invereshie House and the River Feshie, and comes out by the steading of Invereshie Home Farm.

Kingussie Shinty Pitch - under water

Torcroy

Chapter 6
The Back Road (B 970)

Leaving Kingussie by the level-crossing over the railway, the road gradually rises on to an embankment with three underpasses. After a prolonged period of heavy rain or rapid snowmelt, the waters of the Spey fill the whole valley, and on those occasions,the nearby shinty pitch (known as "the Dell") is covered by water. Significantly the only building is on stilts and the pavilion is some distance away - opposite the Secondary School.

The game of shinty has had a long history. The following account was written by a local minister in 1839 and published in the (New) Statistical Account -

"There is one amusement, to which we are called on to allude. It is called camac or shinty matches. It is conducted as follows : A gentleman announces that he is to give a shinty play, on a certain day, in a certain place. The meaning of this announcement is that a certain quantity of whisky is to be distributed, at the place, to the players and spectators. The quantity of whisky provided on these occasions varies, according to the wealth, the liberality, or the vanity of the donors, from four to ten, or perhaps fourteen imperial gallons. Hundreds of people, old and young, gather together on those occasions, and the scene is closed, in many instances, by drunkenness, fighting, and bloodshed. This practice is most injurious to the morals of the people, and ought certainly to be discontinued by the gentry."

By the end of the 19th Century, the rules of shinty were standardised, and whisky was no longer an essential part of the proceedings. Significantly, Kingussie was the first winner of the Camanachd Cup in 1896. ("Caman" is the name of the shinty stick). There is great rivalry between Kingussie and Newtonmore; and it is generally expected that at least one of the teams plays in the final of "the Cup".

In October 1861 Queen Victoria crossed "a long wooden bridge over the Spey" which had only recently been constructed. When the water is low, the remains of that bridge can still be seen. In 1897, that bridge was replaced by an iron bridge which survived until 2015. Previously, General Wade's road had forded the river. John Thomson's *Atlas of Scotland* (1832) shows the ford a few yards downstream of the present bridge, and a branch road leading further downstream where there was a ferry.

Over the Spey, and under the A9, we climb up to Ruthven Steading. The village of Ruthven was sited around here and along the ridge as far as the present car-park. Ruthven was at a strategic point as the ancient routes from Perthshire, namely Comyn's Road and the Minigaig, and General Wade's road over Drumochter all converged on this community.

From Ruthven, the first part of the Minigaig can easily be followed. The track begins at a gate behind the car park, and passes almost immediately through a narrow pass down to the long abandoned township of Braeruthven. After about two miles, as one nears the top of a ridge, the paths divide... the traditional route continuing over the moor in a south westerly direction. The more popular alternative is to take a south easterly branch, which drops down to Glentromie Lodge; and return by Tromie Bridge, or across the moor to Torcroy.

When a bridge was built over the Spey to the south of Newtonmore at Ralia in 1765, the importance of the village of Ruthven began to decline; and its fate was sealed when the modern town of Kingussie was laid out in 1799. Around 1900, it was still possible to identify the outlines of many of the buildings, but now, all trace of the township has disappeared.

The ruins of Ruthven Barracks occupy a historic site. It is said that the Comyns, the first Lords of Badenoch, had their seat there in 1230, that it became a stronghold of the Wolf of Badenoch in the 14th century, and that about 1590, the Earl of Huntly built a new castle on the site. After the Jacobite Rising of 1715, the Castle was purchased by the Government, and a spacious barracks erected between 1718 and 1721.

In 1734, General Wade added the stable buildings to the rear. In August, 1745, the soldiers who were quartered here joined General Cope while on his route to Inverness, leaving only a Sergeant Molloy and a dozen men. In the following month, the Sergeant and his men successfully resisted the attempts of 200 Jacobites to capture the Barracks. However, early in 1746 the Highland army that had returned from Derby, was equipped with cannon and after a short siege, the small garrison capitulated. After Culloden, the Highlanders regrouped at Ruthven, determined to continue the struggle; but here they received from Prince Charles an order to disperse. Before doing so, the Highlanders set the Barracks on fire, and the buildings have remained as a ruin to this day. Notwithstanding this, Ensign Hector Munro had his headquaters here in his search for Cluny; and the Hanoverian Government continued to appoint someone as barrack-master, the last being John Macpherson of Invertromie, then styled "of Inverhall". This practice came to an end in 1792, when the ruin was acquired by the Duke of Gordon. It might perhaps be mentioned that there are ruins of very similar barracks at Bernera, near Glenelg, on the old road to Skye. These barracks survived the Jacobite Rising, and they were still occupied by a sergeant and a few soldiers when Dr. Johnston and James Boswell passed in 1773.

Beyond Ruthven, the farm on the right bears the name Gordonhall *(Lag-an-Notair* - the Notary's Hollow), this being the residence of the Duke of Gordon's factor, at the time when the Duke of Gordon was the principal landowner in the area, and where the rents used to be collected for the Gordon estates.

The road then climbs out of the flood plain up to the RSPB car park and the small community of Torcroy where there was a smithy. In Meta Scarlett's *In The Glens Where I Was Young*, there is a photograph of a wall opposite the houses showing the remains of a cruck, a traditional form of roof-timber built ino the stone wall. Since that photograph was taken, the timber has all gone, merely leaving a gap in the stone. Meta Scarlett relates in her book that behind Torcroy was the Wart Well, a small loch which had medicinal qualities in that the regular washing of hands in the water would remove any warts.

A particular feature of this area is the number of aspen trees, which rustle audibly, even in a gentle breeze.

After leaving Torcroy, there is a track to the left leading to the former farmhouse and steading of Invertromie. The Macphersons of Invertromie were an ancient family, having received a Charter from the Marquis of Huntly, in 1638. There was no mansion house, such as was associated with most Highland estates. Eventually, Hugh Macpherson of Invertromie became indebted to Captain John Macpherson of Ballachroan; and in 1794 the lands were sold to Alexander, the 4th Duke of Gordon on behalf of his illegitimate son, Major George Gordon. Major Gordon was known to the Duchess of

River Tromie - in flood

Speyside Distillery

Gordon as "The Duke's George," to distinguish him from "My George"—her son, George, Marquis of Huntly. Major George Gordon later became Inspector General of Foreign Corps, and in 1835 he sold Invertromie to George Macpherson Grant of Invereshie. The surrounding land is now in the ownership of the RSPB.

Continuing on the B970, a patch of snow can usually be seen, high up on the escarpment beyond Glen Feshie. The hollow holding this snow is known as *Ciste Mhearad*, Margaret's Kist, Chest, or Coffin. Tradition has it that a certain Margaret, who had been jilted by a Mackintosh, died here in her mad wanderings, after having cursed the particular family of Mackintoshes to sterility. An alternative story is that a Glen Feshie maiden loved a youth who had committed some crime. The local laird ordered that he be hanged, and refused her pleas of clemency. In her grief for the loss of her lover she committed suicide on the hill, and the snow is her shroud.

The road takes a turn and narrows at Tromie Bridge - two and a half miles out from Kingussie. The bridge crosses a gorge, and the surrounding rocks are a favourite picnic area. The original bridge was built in 1728 by Peter Macglashen, a mason from Blair Atholl, at a cost of £36 13/4d. It was eight feet wide and was financed by the Parish of Kingussie. (At this time, General Wade was building his road from Fort William to Inverness, but had not then started any of his roads in Badenoch). The bridge was widened and repaired in 1832.

About half a mile downstream of the bridge, there is an enclosure which is an ancient burial ground. On the 1:25000 Ordnance Survey Map, this graveyard is given the name *Cille nan Ceatharnach*. This has been variously translated as the "Chapel or churchyard of the common man". However, the authenticity of this name must be open to doubt as all the other ancient burial grounds in Badenoch have an association with some Celtic Saint. Indeed, Thomas Sinton, in The Poetry of Badenoch (1906) refers to "the chapel-yard of St Colman — *Cladh Machalmaig*" and tells the story about the widow of a Macpherson of Invertromie who was buried there. The widow was then obliged to marry a tenant farmer on the other side of the valley, but she continued to mourn her first love and would climb to the heights behind Kingussie to survey the scene of her early married life. Meta Scarlett in her book on the District, also gives the burial ground the more credible name *Cladh mo Chalmaig* adding that her forebears from Lynaberack, some miles up Glen Tromie, were all buried here. All the gravestones are now weathered or covered in grass, but recently it was possible to read on one of the stones the place name "Croft Martin" - an ancient croft now within the village of Insh.

Immediately beyond Tromie Bridge, a rough track leads off to the right – and that diversion is described in the next Chapter (Chapter 7).

Continuing on the B970 for about 400 yards, a gate on the left merely states "Speyside Distillery", the name having been taken from an earlier distillery which once stood behind the Duke of Gordon Hotel in Kingussie. 18th century maps identify the site as "Millton". Tromie Mill, as it became known, was a meal mill, and for more than a hundred years, it was tenanted by the same family. In the 1950s George Christie, purchased the Mill along with the surrounding farm (Dell of Killiehuntly) and the mansionhouse of Old Milton. He employed Alex Fairlie of Reswallie, near Forfar, to restore the surrounding drystane dykes, and then to erect singlehanded, the building which now accommodates the Distillery. Production of malt whisky only began in 1990; and although it is one of the smallest distilleries in Scotland, it produces the equivalent of half a million bottles of whisky every year. Exceptionally, this distillery does not have a Visitors' Centre. George Christie died in 2012, and the Speyside Distillery company was acquired by Harvey's of Edinburgh, a family business with a tradition of nearly 250 years in the whisky industry. The present member of the family is John Harvey McDonough.

Opposite the Distillery, a steep road climbs up to the village of Drumguish ("the ridge of the pine trees"). Drumguish is a relatively young village. It does not appear in Thomson's Atlas of Scotland of 1832; but shortly after that date, the crofters in the neighbouring township of Killiehuntly, were required to vacate their traditional lands to make way for sheep-farming. Unlike the clearances in the north and west of the Highlands, these crofters were allowed to settle here at what had previously been uncultivated land, and to create new crofts. Only a nominal rent was charged on the understanding that a realistic rent would be paid as soon as each field was cleared. Understandably, the crofters never completed the work, leaving a heap of stones in the corner of each field; and as a result, the rents remained at a nominal amount until the Invereshie Estate sold the lands to the individual crofters in 1953. Throughout the latter part of the 19th Century and the early 20th Century, the community prospered, with many of the crofters having outside employment. At one time, there were two grocers' shops; and Drumguish still had its own shinty team even after the Second World War. However, most of the housing was sub-standard, and with a lack of modern services, the population diminished to a low point around 1973 when there was less than ten residents. Since that time, the availability of piped water and modern building methods, coupled with the availability of building land, has allowed the village to expand to its present population - with only a few houses now being available for holiday letting.

At the crossroads in Drumguish is an ancient ash tree; and it is said that Drumguish will continue to prosper so long as the ash tree survives. Opposite the ash tree is the house that was occupied between 1944 and 1947 by the naturalist, Richard Perry. In his *In the High Grampians* (1948) he describes the inhabitants at that time and their way of life; and he gives a vivid account of walking over to Glen Feshie, climbing the escarpment and exploring the Cairngorm plateau... and returning on the same day. Another author associated with Drumguish was Meta Scarlett. Her grandfather, and her father Duncan MacBean were successively the tenants of the neighbouring farm of Killiehuntly. In her *In the Glens Where I Was Young*, Meta describes the life on the farm until her father retired in 1947. For many years after, Meta lived and worked in Edinburgh, but had the use of an outhouse adjacent to one of the cottages in Lower Drumguish, and this was her base for her continued interest in the district. Sadly, the cottage and the adjacent building have both been demolished.

The crossroads at Drumguish is indeed a meeting of the ways – particularly popular with walkers and mountain bikers. To the south, the old road to Glen Feshie; and east and west, the old road, now designated the Badenoch Way, and to become the extension of the Speyside Way. The track to the east leads to the township of Inveruglass. This was the only community in this area identified in Blaeu *Atlas of Scotland* published in 1654. Until recently, there was one croft and two other traditional cottages at Inveruglass: now it is a thriving community, mostly of modern housing.

Reverting to the B970, two miles from Tromie Bridge takes one to the village of Insh - a mixture of older cottages and modern bungalows - extending for nearly a mile along both sides of the road. It may appear strange that the village bears the name of Insh although is quite distant from Loch Insh and Insh Church. The explanation is that the crofters in Glen Feshie were cleared from their lands some time after 1830. The crofters were allowed to settle here and they called their community "Newtown of Insh" after the name of the Parish. However, the first part of the name soon dropped out of usage. Previously, there had only been two small holdings in the area - Sollerie and Croftmartin - and these names survive in the names of present-day houses.

At the end of the 19th century, Insh still had an hotel and shops. There had been 80 pupils at the school in 1840; but by 1875, there was less than half that number. The school roll was reduced to 22 in 1937, and by 1942, there were only 12 pupils. The school closed in 1947. Until recently, there was still a Post Office in the village. In 1843, at the time of the Disruption in the Church of Scotland, some of the parishioners left the parish church at Loch Insh and held their own services in the open air at this new village. A lay preacher, Donald Cattanach, walked every Sunday from Newtonmore to take the service. Eventually, the local landowner built a small church with an iron roof, and a ship's bell was installed on the gable. The roof has since been slated, and services continue to be held on the third Sunday of the month. The church is always open.

The road now climbs to its highest point passing the farm of Lynchlaggan (another "Laggan"!). The elevated view looks down on the great expanse of meadow land, extending some four miles from Kingussie to Loch Insh, and with a breadth of up to two miles. Within this low ground, the Spey flows with extreme sluggishness, its course being traced by the high embankments that wind along on each side. Also visible is the network of drainage canals which were excavated to reduce the water table. Until recent times these canals were kept free of silt and with the water table being kept low, an immense quantity of natural grass was cut and preserved every year.

After a further mile, the road turns sharply to the left. The road to the right leads up Glen Feshie, and that route is described in Chapter 8. Overlooking this junction is Insh House. The building was originally designed by Thomas Telford, and was the manse for the parish. Behind Insh House is the farm of Balnespick, a name that often appears in historical documents connected with Badenoch from the 13th century. The Gaelic equivalent *bail* (town or residence) and *eashuig* (bishop) suggesting a connection with the Bishopric of Moray.

Continuing on the B970, there is a fascinating feature on the dry stone wall (on the right of the road) which incorporates a series of raised stones with a "cut-out". These cut-outs accommodated horizontal logs which gave the wall the necessary height to exclude deer. A similar wall can also be seen at Killiehuntly, adjacent to the road up Glen Tromie.

A short distance beyond at the growing community of Milehouse, we meet the road from Kincraig, already described in Chapter 5. Beyond this road junction, and among the trees on the right is Ardgeal, a new venture developed by the Highland Small Communities Housing Trust - begun in 2009 with the support of the National Forest Land Scheme.

Half a mile further, there is a Forestry Commission car park from where one can access a unique collection of carvings, scattered among the conifer wood and the old walled garden of Invereshie House. Frank Bruce was born in 1931 in the fishing village of St Combs, near Fraserburgh. He was more interested in the natural beauty of his surroundings; and his love of the Highland environment led him to settle in Aviemore in the 1960s. In 1965, he began sculpting figurative carvings in sandstone and local wood and in 2007, the Forestry Commission agreed to give the carvings their present resting place. Frank died in 2009.

From the car park, it is only a short distance to Feshie Bridge. The twin arched bridge was built in 1786 at the instigation of the then Duke of Gordon. It was so well built that it withstood the flood of August 1829 when the water level was three feet above the keystone. On the right of the bridge is the established right of way through Glen Feshie and Glen Geldie to Braemar. This track follows close to the river and provides an opportunity to look into the gorge immediately above the bridge. Thereafter, the track leads to a disused quarry and then open farmland before the track meets up with the public road south of Balintean.

Beyond the bridge, our road climbs steeply, levelling out at the junction with the other road into Glen Feshie. The B970 then enters the extensive Inshriach Forest. Traditionally, this was the lands of Dalnavert, occupied by a family of Shaws - who were tenants of successive Chiefs of the Clan Mackintosh. About a mile and a half along the road, a sign "Dalnavert" precedes a small community of Forestry Commission houses. An unsurfaced road to the left takes one down to Dalnavert farmhouse and and a unique community established in 1982 when an agricultural co-operative of seven

Frank Bruce Sculptures

members acquired 150 acres, each member being allocated 3.5 acres on which to build a dwellinghouse, with the remaining 120 acres being farmed on a communal basis. Over the years, they gradually improved the land - ditching, draining, fencing, fertilising and sowing – and have built up a herd of 30 Aberdeen Angus. Other ventures have included the growing of heathers and a brown trout fishery.

In May 2010, a cairn was unveiled in Dalnavert to the memory of Sir John A Macdonald, the first Prime Minister of Canada, whose parents came from the district, his mother being of the Shaw family of Dalnavert.

Returning to the B970, a further mile takes the traveller to Inshriach House, built in 1906 as a shooting lodge. In 1938, Jack Drake, a retired army officer, whose family owned the surrounding estate, established an Alpine Garden which still bears his name. Immediately beyond this nursery, a signpost for Rothiemurchus Estate signified that this is the furthest extent of Badenoch.

Suggested walk

The Badenoch Way and the proposed line of the extension to the Speyside Way both shadow the B970 from Loch Insh back to Tromie Bridge. An attractive cicular route is to begin at Drumguish, heading south in the direction of Glen Feshie for about a mile, then turning left at an obvious crossroads; and following a Forestry road for about two miles, coming out at the far end of the village of Insh. It is at this point that the Badenoch Way briefly touches the B970... and the Badenoch Way then provides a scenic return route through Inveruglass and back to Drumguish.

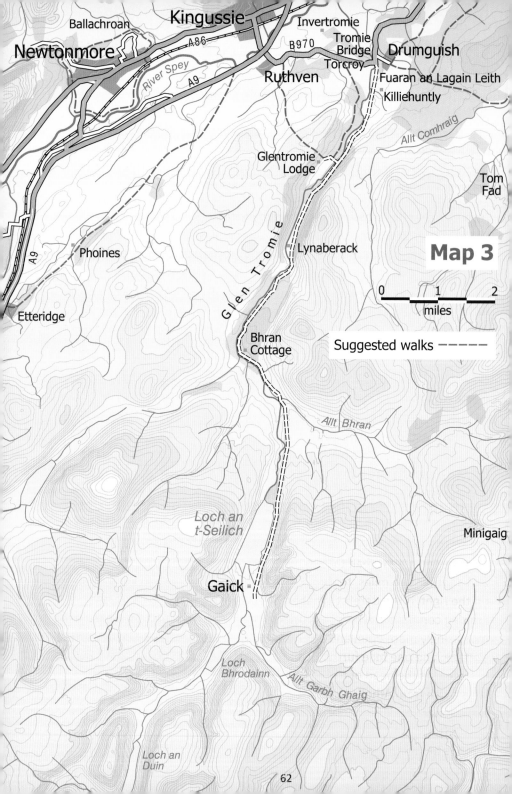

Ballachroan
Kingussie
Invertromie
Tromie
Bridge
Drumguish
Newtonmore
A86
Torcroy
Fuaran an Lagain Leith
River Spey
A9
Ruthven
Killiehuntly
B970
Allt Comhraig

Glentromie
Lodge
Tom
Fad

Map 3

Glen Tromie
Lynaberack

A9
Phoines

0   1   2
miles

Etteridge

Bhran
Cottage
Suggested walks – – – –

Allt Bhran

Loch an
t-Seilich
Minigaig

Gaick

Loch
Bhrodainn
Allt Garbh Ghaig

Loch an
Duin

62

Chapter 7
Glen Tromie

The Estate at the head of Glen Tromie is known as Gaick. The 11 miles of private road to Gaick Lodge are very accessible for the cyclist and it is assumed that the visitor will adopt this means of transport, especially if it is intended to explore the head of the Glen.

Turning right after crossing Tromie Bridge (chapter 6), a short distance takes us to the junction of the old road from Drumguish. This point is identified as Fuaran an Lagain Leith – the "Spring of the grey hollow". Prior to the use of fertiliser, the water surfacing here had the reputation of being the source of the purest water in Badenoch. William Roy's map (1747-1752) shows a township by the name of "Laganlia" in this area, and the name is written as "Lagganleath" in John Thomson's Atlas (1832): this was probably one of the crofting communities which were subsequently cleared to establish the farm of Killiehuntly.

Beyond the next junction, Killiehuntly House can be seen – at one time the residence of a historic Macpherson family. Prior to 1914, Killiehuntly farm employed a grieve, a byre-man, a horseman and a boy, who all lived in bothies; and there were in addition two shepherds and another boy on the hill. There was a dairy and 18 milking cows, two Clydesdales and a pony to pull the governess cart. However, such has been the depression in the agricultural industry, that the farm was latterly run single-handed with no staff. It is now owned by the proprietor of Glenfeshie Estate.

A further mile and a half takes us to the bridge leading to Glentromie Lodge; and another two miles, to the modern Lynaberack Lodge. Beyond the Lodge on the right, is the derelict Lynaberack Cottage, the only remnant of a crofting community which supported a bobbin factory. The Glen becomes increasingly more open and after three more miles, there is the ruin of Bhran Cottage; and one mile further, a bridge over the Allt Bhran and the keeper's cottage. At the head of the Bhran is the Minigaig Pass – the 17th century road north from Atholl. However, during the winter months the high elevation frequently rendered the Minigaig impassable as drifting snow and blizzards engulfed the exposed track, and on one occasion, a company of soldiers heading north to Ruthven Barracks was lost in adverse weather. It is therefore not surprising that when General Wade began his new road from Dunkeld to Inverness in 1728, he preferred the longer but less exposed route through the Drumochter Pass. The Minigaig continued to provide passage for many years after Wade's road opened and remained popular with drovers unwilling to pay the tolls at Drumochter. The Dumfries-born engineer Thomas Telford also considered building a modern road over the Minigaig but he was dissuaded by the elevation; and subsequent roads north – including the present day A9 – have all followed Wade through Drumochter. As a result, the Minigaig is now only a challenging recreational route for walkers and mountain-bikers.

The bridge over the Bhran leads into Gaick Estate, one of the most remote areas in the Scottish Highlands. The Estate was bought by Sir George Macpherson Grant of Ballindalloch from the 5th Duke of Gordon in 1830. The road up Glen Tromie now begins to climb, and after a mile and a half, one comes to the hydro electric dam – the start of the Tummel/Garry scheme - the water being diverted by a series of dams, tunnels and aqueducts, (with the final power station at Pitlochry). Behind the dam is Loch an t-Seilich, and beyond the head of the Loch, two miles from the dam, is Gaick Lodge.

Describing Gaick Estate in 1895, Augustus Grimble observed that

"Edward Ormiston, the head forester, most ably presides, for no gentleman could wish a better, bolder, more brilliant stalker, or pleasanter companion on the hill."

Edward Ormiston was the father of Ewen Ormiston, referred to in Chapter 10.

An account of the life of Captain John Macpherson of Ballachroan, the "Black Officer" appears in Chapter 10. The events leading to his death are graphically described by Thomas Sinton in *The Poetry of Badenoch* (1906) -

"And so it came about that on Monday the 30th December, 1799, Captain Macpherson took his departure for Gaick, accompanied by four attendants, with the purpose of returning on the following Friday, bringing home a supply of venison to garnish a Christmas feast on Monday, the 6th January. As the veteran sportsman was about to ride away from the door of

Ballachroan, one of his servants, old Bell Campbell, whom I knew well, used to tell us how she took off one of her garters and with it fastened his plaid more closely about his shoulders, little thinking that in the course of a few days she would help to lay out his remains.

The weather, which had been very settled for some days, continued calm and frosty until Wednesday evening, when a terrific snowstorm set in. For forty-eight hours the storm continued with unabated fury until the afternoon of Friday, when it gradually subsided, leaving the air clear and cold, and the whole surface of the country covered with an immense depth of snow.

Friday night set in, but Captain Macpherson and his attendants returned not to relieve the anxieties of their friends, who, next morning, despatched a messenger to Gaick to obtain information as to their fate. At Lynaberack, the messenger ascertained that a terrible catastrophe had occurred. The hunting bothy and its unfortunate occupants lay buried beneath a great mass of snow. The messenger returned in haste to Ballachroan, and, next day being Sunday, a dozen men set out from the Church of Kingussie for the scene of the disaster. They made considerable progress in clearing away the snow that lay over the site of the bothy, but daylight failing them, they were forced to take their way home. The country being thoroughly roused, many persons resorted to Gaick to assist in recovering the remains of the unfortunate huntsmen. But it was not until Wednesday that four corpses, which had been discovered, were conveyed to the Strath. So keen was the frost, that the rough deal coffins which contained the bodies, stuck fast to the ground, whenever the bearers laid them down for a few minutes, to rest on their toilsome journey. It was not until several months after this, that a passing foxhunter discovered the fifth body, in a wreath of snow about two or three hundred yards from the site of the bothy."

How the tale developed over the next hundred years, is a story in itself.

In the January 1800 issue of *The Scots Magazine* – the same magazine that is still published today, there appeared the following report –

"We are sorry to hear from Aberdeen that Major Macpherson of Lorick, and other four gentlemen who were out along with him shooting wild-fowl, on the Duke of Gordon's grounds, between Strathspey and Badenoch, having unfortunately perished in the violent storm of snow, which did so much damage by sea and land on Thursday the 2d current. They had retired for shelter to an old cot-house about 16 miles distant from any town, and which was blown down upon them by the fury of the wind. The bodies of Major Macpherson and other three of them were found under the ruins; that of the fifth gentleman was found on the outside of the cottage".

The designation of "Major" and the reference to "Lorick" would appear to be errors, especially as the Black Officer was properly identified as "Captain John Macpherson, Balechroan" on his headstone in St Columba's Churchyard in Kingussie.

Then on 9 May 1800, Anne McVicar Grant, wife of the Minister of Laggan, wrote to a friend -

"I have not leisure to describe to you the dreadful fate of Captain Macpherson of Ballochroan, who, with four others, set out before Christmas to hunt for deer in a chase of the Duke of Gordon's, between this country and Athol. There was a shooting-lodge or cottage, of great strength and solidity, built in that place to shelter the Duke on his summer excursions. There the hunters repaired every night to sleep, having provided fire and food to keep them comfortable for the three days they were to remain. But on the third evening, December 2d, there came on a stormy night; next morning, the father of one of the young men of the Captain's party, went up to see how they fared, but could not see even the house, the roof, timber, and every stone of which had been carried more than two hundred yards distance. The whole country was summoned out to discover and bring home the mortal remains, and the Captain and his associates were found dead, covered with snow, where the house had stood. The story is almost miraculous, and every one hereabout was filled with superstitious horror. We account for it from a whirlwind or avalanche. You can have no idea what a gloom has overspread us; Mr. Grant was always partial to him. There are so many tender, as well as strange circumstances involved in this dismal tale, that the mind cannot shake off the impression."

James Hogg the "Ettrick Shepherd" (who regularly travelled through Badenoch) observed that "in every mountainous district of Scotland, to this day, a belief in supernatural agency prevails..." and he claimed that the events surrounding the death of the Black Officer influenced Sir Walter Scott in his ballad of *Glenfinglas*. These verses first appeared in M G Lewis' *Tales of*

Wonder (1801), and in a footnote, Scott added –

"The simple tradition upon which the preceding stanzas are founded, runs as follows. While two Highland hunters were passing the night in a solitary bothy... and making merry over their venison and whisky, one of them expressed a wish that they had pretty lasses to complete their party. The words were scarcely uttered, when two beautiful young women, habited in green, entered the hut, dancing and singing. One of the hunters was seduced by the siren who attached herself particularly to him, to leave the hut: the other remained, and, suspicious of the fair seducers, continued to play upon a trump, or Jew's harp, some strain consecrated to the Virgin Mary. Day at length came, and the temptress vanished. Searching in the forest, he found the bones of his unfortunate friend, who had been torn to pieces and devoured by the fiend into whose toils he had fallen."

In 1810, James Hogg began publishing *The Spy*, a weekly paper of "literary amusement and instruction"; and in an early issue, he set out the story surrounding "the miraculous death of Major Macpherson", his account describing how the "Major" and some friends went out to hunt in the middle of that tremendous range of mountains which rise between Atholl and Badenoch. In the afternoon they retired to a little bothy or resting lodge, that stood by the side of a rough mountain stream, and having meat and drink, they abandoned themselves to mirth and jollity. When their hilarity was at the highest pitch, a stranger appeared. The stranger beckoned to the Major, who followed him instantly out of the bothy. The stranger appeared to threaten Macpherson, and when they parted, the stranger disappeared. However, the countenance of the Major was so visibly altered that the mirth of the party was marred for the rest of the excursion. At the end of the same week, Macpherson insisted on a further expedition. On this occasion, only one solitary dog returned, wounded and maimed. The search party found the bothy torn from its foundations and the dead bodies of the whole party lying scattered about suggesting some supernatural agency as the probable cause.

Offenbach's Opera *The Tales of Hoffmann*, has a remote and rather surprising connection. The hero of the Opera was Theodore Hoffmann, a romantic author of fantasy and horror, who died in 1822. Five years after Hoffmann's death, Sir Walter Scott contributed an article to the first issue of the *Foreign Quarterly Review*, entitled "On the Supernatural in Fictitious Composition;

and particularly on the works of Theodore William Hoffmann". As an illustration of the supernatural, Scott enlarged on James Hogg's account. Scott attributed the tale to a schoolmaster in the neighbourhood of Rannoch; relating that Captain Macpherson -

"was popularly reported to be a man of no principles, rapacious, and cruel; that he had got money by procuring recruits from the Highlands, an unpopular mode of acquiring wealth; and that, amongst other base measures for this purpose, he had gone so far as to leave a purse upon the road, and to threaten the man who had picked it up with an indictment for robbery, if he did not enlist."

According to Scott, the previous event had occurred "about a month before"; and he added

"One evening after dusk, when Captain Macpherson was in the bothy, some of his party that were standing before the door saw a fire blazing on the top of the hill which rises in front of it. They were much surprised to see a fire in such a solitary place, and at such a time, and set out to inquire into the cause of it, but when they reached the top of the hill, there was no fire to be seen!"

Scott gave a graphic account of the devastation following on the fatal event, adding that

"One of the bodies, indeed, was found at a distance of many yards from the bothy; another of the men was found upon the place where the bothy had stood, with one stocking off, as if he had been undressing; Captain Macpherson was lying without his clothes, upon the wretched bed which the bothy had afforded, his face to the ground, and his knees drawn up."

Concluding that the extraordinary wreck of the building had led the common people to ascribe it to a supernatural power.

Contemporaries of Sir Walter Scott were the brothers John Carter Allen and Charles Manning Allen, who claimed to be legitimate grandchildren of Prince Charles Edward Stuart. Lord Lovat gave them the use of a hunting lodge; and in 1848, they published under their assumed names John Sobieski Stuart and Charles Edward Stuart, *Lay of the Deer Forest. With sketches of olden and modern deer-hunting.* Within that publication, there is an even more detailed account of the Gaick Catastophe attributing their version of the story to a contemporary who was well acquainted with the parties who perished. The Black Officer's companions were named for the first time as Donald MacGillivray, John MacPherson, Duncan MacPharlan and a man named Grant; and it was said that MacPharlan's body was not found until all the snow had melted, when he was discovered at a considerable distance from the bothy. The Stuarts acknowledged that the awful character of the destruction in Gaick had excited superstitious imagination. Some writers suggested that the house had been torn to pieces in a vortex of thunder and lightning, launched by the vengeance of Heaven against sinners; others attributed the destruction to a whirlwind raised by the devil.

In 1900, Alexander Macpherson, lawyer and banker in Kingussie, published a pamphlet *Captain John Macpherson – A Counter-blast*. In the Introduction, he refers to the intention to erect a commemorative cairn, and the proceeds of sale of the pamphlet contributed towards the cost of the cairn at Gaick which was set up in 1902.

The track continues for a further three miles beyond Gaick Lodge. A sign tells you that this is "Domingo's Road" - but this name has no historical tradition, being so called after the co-owner of the Estate in the late 20th Century. Within the first mile, it is necessary to ford the Allt Gharbh Ghaig. It is here that Comyn's Road came over the hills from the South. It is said that the Road was built by David Comyn, Lord of Badenoch, to transport a particularly fine ale from an inn near the Blair Atholl to his Badenoch home. Comyn's Road was superseded by the Minigaig in the 17th Century.

Beyond the Allt Gharbh Ghaig is Loch Bhrodainn, and finally Loch an Duin, which straddles the narrow pass leading to the Edendon to Dalnacardoch.

It might perhaps be added that Gaick was regarded throughout Badenoch as a place of evil omen - a veritable haunt of horrors - long before the disaster which overwhelmed the Black Officer and his companions. Affleck Grey, in his *Legends of the Cairngorms* (1987) tells us that it was beneath the waters of Loch Bhrodainn that Calum Ban's hound and the famous white hind of Ben Alder disappeared. On the rocky slopes of near Loch an t-Seilich, Walter Comyn was torn in pieces by eagles, and it was also in Gaick that Muireach Maclain experienced the last proof of the Witch of Laggan's versatility in the black art.

Suggested walk

For the walker, an excellent introduction to Glen Tromie is to follow the ancient route from Ruthven described in the previous chapter. Until recently, this path ended at the back door of Glentromie Lodge! By arrangement with the owner, a rather boggy diversion takes one down to a style adjacent to a cottage. It is possible to climb over this style, leading to the bridge over the Tromie and then to follow the motor road down to Tromie Bridge.

However a more attractive route is to turn left, taking the track below the kennels, which leads down the left bank of the Tromie and then crosses the moor, coming out on the B970 shortly before Torcroy.

Chapter 8
Glen Feshie

This is one of the great glens of Scotland, stretching from Aberdeenshire to the valley of the Spey. Looking at a map, it will be seen that the River Feshie has already flowed east for several miles before it approaches the Aberdeenshire county boundary, and then turns almost about on itself. Following downstream, the open moorland of the march, gradually narrows with escarpments on both sides and giant juniper in the valley floor, then opening out to extensive grassland, before eventually being swallowed up in expanses of pine forest, some native, but mostly coniferous plantations.

Glen Feshie is of particular significance in that with the Geldie in Aberdeenshire, it provides a relatively low level route through the Cairngorms. About three miles south of the Geldie, is the flat topped mountain An Scarsoch which was reputedly a gathering point for drovers taking cattle south, perhaps predating the trysts of Crieff and Falkirk - with many of these drovers having come through Glen Feshie. The droving continued until the mid 1800s, by which time the railways provided a quicker and safer means of transporting livestock. In building his roads through Drumochter and over the Corrieyairick, General Wade followed existing drove roads, and it is not surprising that he also looked at the possibility of a road through Glen Feshie. On his instructions, there was prepared

"A Plan of the Country where the New Intended Road is to be made from the Barrack at Ruthven . Badenoch to InverCall in BreaMar. Extracted from my Surveys made for the Duke of Gordon and such Information as coud be had from Major Caulfield about the same 1735.   by Joseph Avery"

J B Salmond's *Wade in Scotland* (1934) reproduced a sketch of this map, and in his narrative, he still contemplated the possibility of a direct road from Braemar to Kingussie. After the Second World War, enthusiasm continued until 1972, when it was ultimately decided that there should be no highway through the Glen.

Queen Victoria recognised the suitability of the Glen as a through route when she set out from Balmoral at about 8 am on 4 September 1860. In her Journal, she describes her experience -

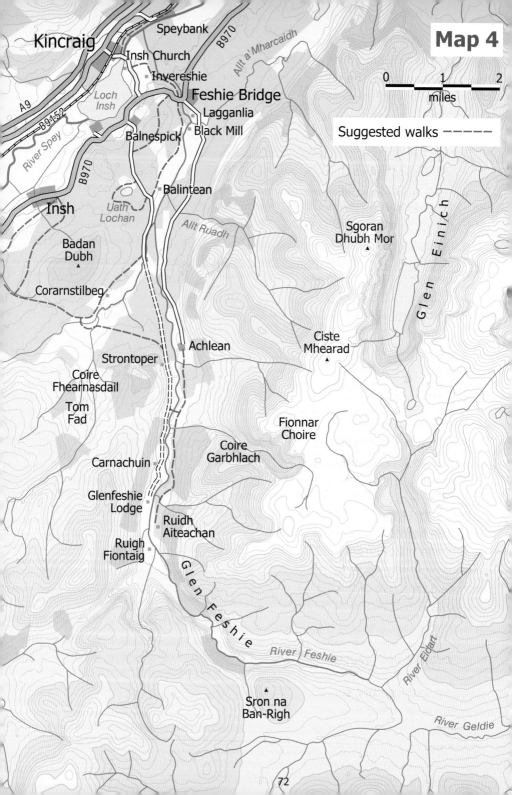

Map 4

0   1   2
miles

Suggested walks − − − − −

Kincraig
Speybank
Insh Church
Invereshie
Feshie Bridge
Lagganlia
Black Mill
Balnespick
Balintean
Loch Insh
A9
B9-152
River Spey
B970
Uath Lochan
Insh
Badan Dubh ▲
Corarnstilbeg
Allt a'Mharcaidh
B970
Allt Ruadh
Sgoran Dhubh Mor ▲
Glen Einich
Ciste Mhearad ▲
Achlean
Strontoper
Coire Fhearnasdail
Tom Fad
Carnachuin
Glenfeshie Lodge
Ruidh Aiteachan
Ruigh Fiontaig
Coire Garbhlach
Fionnar Choire
Glen Feshie
River Feshie
River Eidart
Sron na Ban-Righ ▲
River Geldie

72

"The Fishie is a fine rapid stream, full of stones. As you approach the glen, which is very narrow, the scenery becomes very fine – particularly after fording the Etchart [the Eidart], a very deep ford. Grant, on his pony, led me through: our men on foot took off their shoes and stockings to get across. From this point, the narrow path winds along the base of the hills of Craig-na-Go'ar – the Rocks of the "Goat Craig"; Craig-na-Caillach; and Stron-na-Barin - "the Nose of the Queen". The rapid river is overhung by rocks, with trees, birch and fir; the hills, as you advance, rise very steeply on both sides, with rich rocks and corries, and occasional streamlets falling from very high – while the path winds along, rising gradually higher and higher. It is quite magnificent!"

The reference to Stron-na-Barin - "the Nose of the Queen", otherwise *Sron na Ban-righ*, recalls one of the numerous traditions as to the origin of the burning of Scottish forests. This particular legend credits Mary Queen of Scots with the destruction of the forest in Glen Feshie. It is said that her husband, on his return from a distant hunting expedition, had asked about the forest before he enquired as to his spouse. She was grievously offended at this slight; and seated on this very hill, she gave orders to set the forest on fire.

Queen Victoria returned the Glen Feshie in 1861, this time on 8 October. On that occasion, the conditions were less attractive, and she relates -

"We had gone on very well for about an hour, when the mist thickened all round, and down came heavy, or at least beating, rain with wind. With the help of an umbrella, and waterproofs and a plaid, I kept quite dry. Dearest Albert, who walked from the time the ground became boggy, got very wet, but was none the worse for it... Brown waded through the Etchart leading my pony; and then two of the others, who were riding together on another pony, dropped the whole bundle of cloaks into the water!"

In July 1967, a Territorial Army platoon erected a footbridge over the Eidart, some distance upstream from the ford.

From the 15th century, successive Earls of Huntly (latterly Dukes of Gordon) were the lords of Badenoch. Gradually, they released their control of Glen Feshie. In 1568, the Chief of the Clan Mackintosh acquired the land to the east of the river, and in the following century, the Macphersons of Invereshie became the owners of the lower lands on the west bank. In 1753, the Macphersons leased upper Glen Feshie. In 1816, the family, having adopted the name "Macpherson Grant", acquired a title to the remainder of the west bank still in the ownership of the Duke of Gordon, but the Macpherson Grants did not acquire the Mackintosh lands on the east side of the river until 1925. Sir George Macpherson Grant, the 5th Baronet, died in 1951 and his Trustees sold the lands of Invereshie, some of it to existing tenants and the remainder to the Forestry Commission. Glenfeshie Estate (upper Glen Feshie) was sold by the Macpherson-Grant family in 1967; and it is now in Danish ownership.

There are two public roads giving access to Glen Feshie. The route on the east bank of the River is favoured by those seeking access to the higher ground. Coming from the direction of Kingussie, this road branches to the right shortly after Feshie Bridge and passes the community of Lagganlia before dropping down to cross the Allt a' Mharcaidh. At one time, this stream formed the boundary between the Rothiemurchus estate, owned by Patrick Grant, and the lands owned by the Mackintosh. A mill, known as the Black Mill, was established on the Mackintosh side of the Allt a' Mharcaidh, and it was claimed by Patrick Grant that water for the Mill was being diverted from the Rothiemurchus Estate. When there was a threat from the Mackintoshes to burn down Patrick's house at the Doune, he called in Rob Roy Macgregor. The Mackintoshes slipped away; and Rob Roy completed his mission by seeing to it that the Mill was destroyed by fire.

After crossing the Allt a' Mharcaidh, the road comes to an airstrip occupied by the Cairngorm Gliding Club. The location is a particular favourite as the rising air downwind of the ridge between Glen Feshie and Glen Einich can cause a "mountain wave", making it possible for gliders to climb to over 20,000 feet.

Continuing on the road, one reaches a wooden bridge where the Allt Ruadh comes tumbling down. Here there is ample parking and a clear track which provides access through the forest and upwards towards the ultimate summit of Sgor Gaoith. However, the preferred route for anyone seeking the tops is to continue on the road to the car park short of Achlean. The road to the sheep farm of Achlean is still public, but there is no suitable parking there, and walkers are encouraged to walk the last half mile of the road. From Achlean, there is an excellent stalkers path which gradually ascends up to the plateau which has Sgoran Dubh Mor (no longer a Munro !) as its summit. An alternative is to skirt round the farm and continue along the bank of the Feshie. After about a mile Coire Garbhlach comes into view – narrow and steep-sided. Within this gorge, a rough path follows the burn upstream, eventually coming to Fionnar Choire on the left, giving easy access up and on to the plateau.

The alternative road, giving access to the west bank of the Feshie, begins at Insh House, seven miles from Kingussie on the B970. The road climbs past Balnespick Farm (Gaelic bail - town or residence and eashuig – Bishop), so named from the connections with the Bishopric of Moray in the 13th century. After about a mile, an unsurfaced road on the right leads to the attractive picnic site and lochs of Uath Lochan "the dread lochs". The name is probably derived from the wild and lonely nature of the situation, also the lochs are near to the Badan Dubh, the "Black Forest" of pines which lies to the south-west. A board walk and adjoining paths makes it possible to walk round the lochs. Towering above the lochs are the rocks of Craig Far-Leitire. A rough track can be found on either side of this hill, enabling one to complete another circuit with outstanding views over the forests of lower Glen Feshie.

Returning to the road, a track branches to the left, leading to Ballintian; and it is here that the right of way from Feshie Bridge joins the road. After a further mile, another track branches to the right, leading into the broad meadows of Coire Fhearnasdail. The house and steading of Corarnstilbeg have recently been demolished but the "corarnstil" part of the name gives a clue to the pronunciation of "Coire Fhearnasdail"! The track continues along the side of the meadow before climbing with a gentle hairpin bend over the Badan Dubh and down to Drumguish. Before leaving Coire Fhearnasdail mention should be made of Tom Fad, sometime a summer sheiling, and later a permanent settlement. It is identified by name in a map produced for General Roy in 1750, and again in Thomson's map of 1832. The name is not replicated on any Ordnance Survey map, but an outline of the ruins appears on the 1:25,000 Pathfinder map. (NN 964 825) Looking from the track, the grass of the extended enclosure can easily be seen. Meta Scarlett, in her *In The Glens Where I Was Young* (1988) related that

"In the 1790's a community of Stewarts lived there but by 1841 the population was reduced to one agricultural labourer, John McLean, with his wife and four children. Its interest lies in the layout, still discernable, of a typical township with the outlines of houses, a very well-preserved kiln of the type used for drying corn, an infield enclosed by a drystone dyke and a circular stell, that is a cattle fold. Though so long abandoned Tom Fad shows up from a distance as a verdant patch of fertility in the surrounding heather. Like most old Highland houses they were beautifully sited. From Tom Fad you can see down Feshie and Spey to Tor Alvie and in the background the smoke of Aviemore."

Returning to the Glen Feshie road, it dips down to cross the Allt Comhraig, and here one must leave any car, as the road is private from this point. However, the walker or cyclist may continue.

After 1½ miles, we come to where the shorter route from Kingussie reaches the glen. In the guidebooks to Badenoch published in the early years of the 20th century, this was identified as an alternative road to Glen Feshie, but the latter section across Coire Fhearnasdail is now only suitable for walkers or mountain bikes.

A brief climb takes one up to a white house, Strontoper – at one time a school – demonstrating that the Glen at one time had a significant population.

A short distance downhill leads to a modern bridge over the Feshie, now the only bridge other than the bridge on the B970. This bridge allows the cyclist the opportunity of a round trip back to Feshie Bridge via Achlean. The bridge is also now the essential crossing of the river for anyone heading through to Braemar, as the bridge at Carnachuin, three miles upstream, was swept away on 3 September 2009. There is still a vehicular ford at Carnachuin, but even when the water is low, it is likely to be knee depth. Half a mile beyond Carnachuin, the motor road ends at Glenfeshie Lodge – built about 1892.

In Chapter 4, there is reference to the family of Alexander, 4th Duke of Gordon and his wife Jane Maxwell, who were married in 1767. The land at Kinrara was given over to Jane as part of a settlement against her unfaithful husband. Jane built the present house at Kinrara and spent much of her family time there. Jane died in 1812, and in 1816, Alexander sold the west side of upper Glen Feshie to Sir George Macpherson Grant of Invereshie, his family having had a lease of the same for more than a century before.

Jane's youngest daughter Georgina, had enjoyed the surroundings so much that she persuaded her husband, John, the Duke of Bedford, to take a lease of the west side of upper Glen Feshie in 1825, and they had a lodge built at Ruigh Fiontaig, about a mile south of the present lodge. Five years later, the Mackintosh was persuaded to lease the east side of the Glen Feshie, and from that time, the whole of the upper part of the Glen came to be known as Glenfeshie Estate.

On the opposite side of the Feshie from the Lodge there is a large area of level ground known at one time as "the Island", and now the location of an open bothy – Ruidh Aiteachan*. Here the Duke and Duchess of Bedford had a number of wooden cottages constructed, which became known as "the Huts"; and at the Huts, the Duchess and her friends had a particularly wild social life. One of the guests was Edwin Landseer (1802 – 1873): he was already a well-known painter when the Duke of Bedford became his patron in 1823. The Duke and Jane, his Duchess, introduced Landseer to Glen Feshie in the autumn 1825, and such was the relationship between them that it is said that Landseer was the father of Jane's youngest daughter Rachel, who was born in June 1826! It should be added that the Duke also had a number of outside relationships. Sir Edwin Landseer (as he became known) accompanied the Bedfords to Glen Feshie practically every year, continuing even after the Duke's death in 1839, until the Duchess herself died in 1853.

Landseer had a particular fondness for painting hunting scenes which began with sketches made whilst he was in Glen Feshie; and many of his famous paintings of the red deer are from this period. In one of the Huts, Landseer made a chalk drawing of a group of deer with a suspicious hind, on the plaster above the fireplace. In another building used as a dining-room, he sketched a stag above a fire-place.

*The present bothy is of a later date, and has no associations with either Georgina, Duchess of Bedford or of Sir Edwin Landseer.

Chimney at Landseer's Hut

In September 1860, Queen Victoria related

"Then we came upon a most lovely spot – the scene of all Landseer's glory – and where there is a little encampment of wooden and turf huts, built by the late Duchess of Bedford... and alas, all falling into decay..."

and in 1861, she added -

"The huts, surrounded by magnificent fir-trees and quantities of juniper-bushes, looked lovelier than ever; we gazed with sorrow at their utter ruin. I felt what a delightful little encampment it must have been, and how enchanting to live in such a spot as this beautiful solitary wood in a glen surrounded by the high hills. We got off, and went into one of the huts to look at a fresco of stags of Landseer's over a chimney piece."

However, as the huts came to be disused, the drawings were left exposed to the damp. In the 1870s, the Mackintosh, who remained the owner of this part of the Estate, erected a new building in order to preserve this precious memento of the great painter's genius. All that now remains is a free standing chimney. High up on the chimney, there are still the traces of two roof lines, one of which may have reflected the roof of Mackintosh's building. The absence of any gable would indicate that the chimney was a part of a timber building. In the early part of the 20th century, traces of one of Landseer's sketches could still be made out on the plaster; and indeed Meta Scarlett recorded that her father took her here shortly after the Second World War, and at that time "alas only rubble remained with faint tinges of colour on the plaster". Sadly, even the plaster has now gone.

In 1851, Landseer was commissioned to paint three pictures for the newly restored House of Commons; but the authorities refused to pay his fee of £150, and Landseer sold the paintings privately. One of these paintings was an evocative depiction of a majestic stag, with the description "Monarch of the Glen". The present owner of the picture is a commercial company with major interests in the production of Scotch Whisky, and the painting is now on permanent loan to the National Museum of Scotland in Chamber Street, Edinburgh. The name of the picture was taken by Sir Compton Mackenzie as the title of a novel published in 1941; and in turn the BBC adopted the same name for a television series between 2000 and 2005 which was largely filmed in and around Badenoch.

Suggested walk

The length of Glen Feshie is such as to require a whole day to explore. However, some of the attraction of Glen Feshie can be experienced by setting off from Feshie Bridge – upstream, with the river on one's left. A broad path leads through woodland and enclosed fields; and after about 1 1/2 miles the track comes to Balintean and then uphill to the public road. Turning left for a few yards, a gated track on the other side of the road leads to a small loch with a bird observatory on the opposite shore. Beyond this loch, a path to the right leads through pine woods to the Uath Lochan picnic site. We are now on an unsurfaced road which leads back to the public road. Turn left, and proceed for about 500 yards to a cottage. At this point turn right on a forestry track with open views over the glen and the escarpment beyond, before dropping down to the B970. Turn right for a few hundred yards back to Feshie Bridge.

Chapter 9
Kingussie to Newtonmore

Over the three miles between Kingussie and Newtonmore, there is a paved walkway/cycle track in addition to the public road. This road became the main highway from Perth to Inverness in 1765 when the Duke of Gordon built a bridge over the Spey at Ralia, on the other side of Newtonmore. The road from Kingussie to Newtonmore was also part of the route taken by the last stagecoach service in Britain. The writer's mother had a particular memory of the coach leaving Kingussie each day. This was at 9 am, the coach reaching Loch Laggan at 12 noon and Tulloch Station at 3 pm - where a traveller would have been able to board a train for Fort William. The corresponding coach left Tulloch at 8.30 am, arriving in Kingussie at 11.50 am. In the Summer months, there was a second coach, leaving Kingussie at 1.10 pm arriving at Tulloch at 5.45 pm. The Highland Railway advertised a return ticket covering both a train journey from various stations in Perthshire to Kingussie and the coach to Loch Laggan (excluding the coachman's fee of one shilling!) - and it was possible to do this double journey in the Summer with a two hour stopover at the Loch, as the second coach left Tulloch at 11.20 am and Loch Laggan at 2 pm, arriving back in Kingussie at 5 pm. The final coach run was in 1915, and in June 2015, there was a re-enactment of this event.

As one leaves Kingussie, there is a small copse of pine trees to the left of the road on a hillock known as An Cnocan Dhubh (the Black Knoll). In the early 19th century, it was here that the Gordon family would preside over any sports gathering that might be held under their auspices.

At the next bend in the road is Pitmain Farm: the name *Pitmeadhan,* meaning "middle township" the first syllable deriving from the Pictish word Pit, meaning "place". The present Pitmain Estate extends westward almost to Newtonmore, to the North of Kingussie beyond the golf course and on the east to include Kerrow. The Macphersons of Pitmain are the oldest cadet branch of Clan Macpherson. They were tenant farmers, never owning any of these lands; and the family left Badenoch in the 18th Century.

John MacLean, who had served in the Scotch Brigade of the Dutch Army, returned to Scotland in 1750 and took over the tenancy of Pitmain Farm.

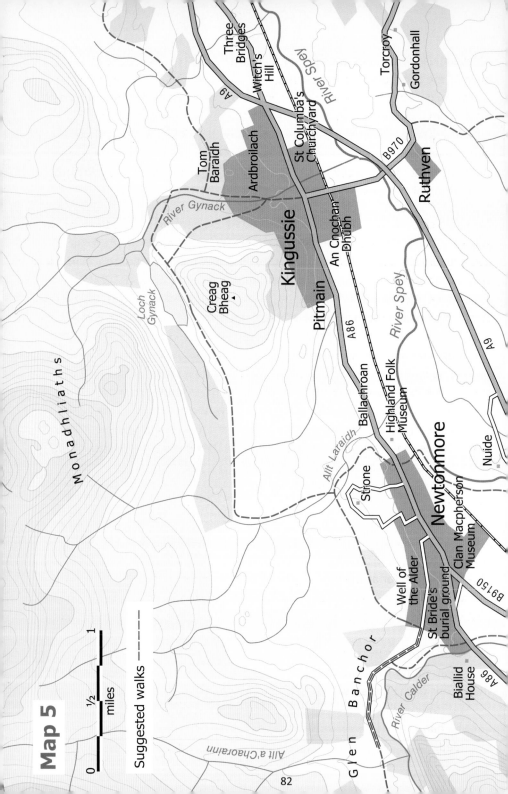

Map 5

Suggested walks - - - - -

0 ½ 1
miles

Monadhliaths

Loch Gynack

River Gynack

Tom Baraidh

Creag Bheag ▲

Three Bridges

Witch's Hill

A9

St Columba's Churchyard

River Spey

Ardbroilach

Torcroy

Gordonhall

B970

Ruthven

Kingussie

An Cnochan Dhubh

Pitmain

A86

River Spey

A9

Ballachroan

Allt Laraidh

Highland Folk Museum

Strone

Newtonmore

Nuide

Clan Macpherson Museum

Well of the Alder

St Bride's burial ground

B9150

Glen Banchor

Biallid House

A86

River Calder

Allt a'Chaorainn

MacLean used his experience from the Netherlands in draining the flood plain of the Spey; and taking advantage of the re-routing of the highway, he established a coaching inn at Pitmain in 1765. MacLean also moved the Post office from Ruthven to Pitmain; hastening the decline of the township of Ruthven. The inn was the venue for the celebration when the Estates of Cluny (having been forfeit after the Jacobite Rising in 1745) were restored to the family in 1784. The celebrated Colonel Thornton recorded the following description of the event -

"At five o'clock dinner was announced, and each gentleman, with the utmost gallantry, handed in his tartan-drest partner. The table was covered with every luxury the vales of Badenoch, Spey, and Lochaber could produce, and a very substantial entertainment it was; game of all kinds, and venison in abundance, did honour to Mr MacLean, who supplied it. I had no conception of any room at Pitmain large enough to dine one-tenth of the party, but found that the apartment we were in, though low, was about fifty feet long, and was only used, being a malt-kiln, on such occasions. When seated, no company at St James's ever exhibited a greater variety of gaudy colours, the ladies being dressed in all their Highland pride, each following her own fancy, and wearing a shawl of tartan: this, contrasted by the other parts of the dress, at candle-light presented a most glaring coup-d'oeil. The dinner being removed, was succeeded by a dessert of Highland fruits, when, I may venture to say, that 'George the Third - and long may he reign!' was drank with as much unfeigned loyalty as ever it was at London: several other toasts were likewise drank with three cheers, and re-echoed by the inferiors of the clan in the area around us. The ladies gave us several very delightful Erse (Gaelic) songs. Nor were the bagpipes silent; they played many old Highland tunes, and, among others, one which is, I am told, the test of a piper's abilities, for at the great meeting of the pipers at Falkirk, those who cannot play it are not admitted candidates for the annual prize given to the best performer. After the ladies had retired, the wine went round plentifully, but, to the honour of the conductor of this festive board, everything was regulated with the utmost propriety; and, as we were in possession of the only room for dancing, we rose the earlier from the table, in compliance with the wishes of the ladies, who in this country are still more keen dancers than those of the southern parts of Britain. After tea, the room being adjusted and the band ready, we returned; and, minuets being by common consent exploded, danced with true Highland spirit a great number of different reels, some of which were danced with the genuine Highland fling, a peculiar kind of cut. It is astonishing how true these ladies all dance to time, and not without grace; they would be thought good dancers in any assembly whatever. At ten o'clock the company repaired to the terrace adjoining to the house to behold as fine a scene of its kind as perhaps ever was exhibited. Bonfires in towns are only simple assemblages of inflammable matter, and have nothing but the cause of rejoicing to recommend them; but here the country people, vying with each other, had gathered together large piles of wood, peat, and dry heather, on the tops of the different hills and mountains, which, by means of signals, being all lighted at the same time, formed a most awful and magnificent spectacle, representing so many volcanos, which, owing to their immense height, and the night being totally dark and serene, were distinctly seen at the distance of ten miles. And, while our eyes were gratified with this solemn view, our ears were no less delighted with the different bagpipes playing round us; when, after giving three cheers to the king, and the same to Mr Pitt, &c, we returned into the ball-room. At one I withdrew, took some refreshment, and then returned home, highly delighted at having passed the day so very agreeably."

Many famous travellers stopped at Pitmain, including Robert Burns, who stayed there in 1787. Elizabeth Grant (of Rothiemurchus), writing of her experience in 1812, observed -

"We never see such inns now: no carpets on the floors, no cushions in the chairs, no curtains to the windows... All the accessories of the dinner were wretched, but the dinner itself, I remember, was excellent; hotch-potch, salmon, fine mutton, grouse, scanty vegetables, bad bread, but good wine."

Lord Cockburn, the Court of Session Judge, was a reluctant visitor in the first half of the 19th century, explaining that "the traveller had to pass two nights on the road between Edinburgh and Inverness, even when going by the fastest public coach, (and) Pitmain was his second house of refuge". In retrospect, Cockburn referred to the Inn at Pitmain as "my old friend"; but then he went on to describe Pitmain as an abominable hostel, and that when the coach arrived -

"the enormous vehicle disgorged a cargo of beasts, clean and unclean, greater than what loaded the ark, and, knowing by experience the advantage of first possession, every monster rushed in and seized whatever he could lay his claws upon - meat, drink, the seat next the fire, the best room, the best bed - and awkwardness or timidity were left to shiver or starve! The moment of the arrival was quite well known, yet the savages of the house, partly from Sawney's natural want of tidiness, and partly from knowing that they had the defenceless wretches in their power, never had anything ready or arranged, but considered the hubbub as showing the importance of the house. Yet the merriest night I ever had was there... It was on that night that an experienced quartermaster, who was missing at the public supper, was found to have secured himself a bed by having taken real, corporeal and actual possession of the first that came, drenched but undressed, and having thus appropriated the prize by spoiling it for anybody else, ate his morsel and drank his jorum as he lay in peace, leaving one dry and well-fed fellow-traveller, who had been sneering during his damp friend's cramming, to sleep on the floor."

Pitmain was also the site of the Pitmain Tryst, an annual cattle market held in the month of September. The sellers were the various landowners and tenant farmers: the buyers were drovers - who carried off their purchase in large herds to the south, either to be privately disposed of, or resold at Falkirk for the English market. In the evening, drovers, landowners and tenant farmers all came together to eat and drink in the large room at Pitmain. Elizabeth Grant related that ladies were invited to this social occasion for the first time in 1814 - not for the dinner, but to prepare tea in another room, which would break up the punch party and allow the larger room to be made ready for dancing.

Until about 1860, St Columba's Fair *(Latha Feill Chaluim Chille)* was held on Midsummers Day in Kingussie. It was always the occasion of a great gathering from around Badenoch, some coming to trade - others for the general amusement of the day. The event in 1838 was particularly memorable. An emigrant ship, bound for Sydney in Australia, was lying off Oban. 76 adults and 57 children from in and around Kingussie had been booked for this sailing ; and it was arranged that they would depart on this particular day - by horse cart to Fort William, and then to their place of embarkation by steamboat.

Thomas Sinton, a native of Badenoch and latterly Minister at Dores, had had first hand accounts of the occasion from a number of near relatives when they described with deep emotion the scenes of heart-rending grief which they witnessed; and he gave the following account in his The Poetry of Badenoch (1906).

"A band of strolling musicians in connection with some entertainment, readily entered into the situation and temper of their assembled patrons at the fair. Playing airs suited to the occasion, and followed by crowds of people, they made their way to the top of Creag Bheag, which commands a view of the whole of Badenoch downwards from Glen Truim. From that height, where a few years before, 'the young men of Kingussie' had erected a cairn in memory of Duke Alexander [the 4th Duke of Gordon], many eyes were turned wistfully to take a last farewell of rauch-loved haunts and homes.

After descending from the Creag Bheag, the emigrants set out on their westward journey, accompanied as far as the old stage-house of Pitmain by relatives and friends. Here, those who were departing for the New World and those who were remaining behind took leave of each other as persons who would never meet again on this side the grave."

The St George set sail on 4 July and reached Sydney more than five months later, on 13 November 1838.

There is no more haunting sound in Badenoch than to hear a Gaelic singer cry out the lament *Gu'm a slan do na fearaibh theid thairis a' chuan*, written by a local resident Donald Campbell *(Domhnull Phail nan oran)*, who had planned to accompany the other emigrants and seek his fortune, but was at the last minute, prevented from travelling. In his volume, Sinton published both the original words and his own translation.

Gu'm a slan do na fearaibh	A health to the fellows,

Gu'm a slan do na fearaibh
Theid thairis a' chuan,
Gu talamh a' gheallaidh,
Far nach fairich iad fuachd.

A health to the fellows,
Who'll cross o'er the sea !
To the country of promise,
Where no cold will they feel.

Gu'm a slan do na mnathan
Nach cluinnear an gearan,
'S ann theid iad gu smearail;
'G ar leantuinn thar 'chuan.

A health to the goodwives !
We'll hear no complaining;
They'll follow us heartily
Over the sea.

'Us na nighneagan boidheach,
A dh' fhalbhas leinn comhladh,
Gheibh daoine ri 'm posadh,
A chuireas or 'nan da chluais.

And the beautiful maidens
Going with us together,—
They'll get husbands to marry,
Who'll give ear-rings of gold.

Gheibh sinn aran 'us im ann,
Gheibh sinn siucar 'us tea ann;
'S cha bhi gainne oirnn-fhìn,
'S an tir 's am bheil buaidh.

We'll get bread and butter,
And sugar and tea there:
We'll experience no want,
In that bountiful land.

'N uair dh' fhagas sinn 'n t-ait' so,
Cha chuir iad mor-mhal oirnn ;
'S cha bhi an Fheila Màrtainn
'Cur naire 'n ar gruaidh.

When we're gone from this country
Our rents will be trifling;
And Martinmas will not
Bring blush to our cheek.

Gu'm fag sinn an tir so,
Cha chinnich aon ni ann ;
Tha 'm buntat' air dol 'dhìth ann,
'S cha chinn iad le fuachd.

We'll depart from this region,
Where nothing will flourish —
The potatoes are ruined,
And won't grow for the cold.

Gheibh sinn crodh agus caoraich
Gheibh sinn cruithneachd air raointean,
'S cha bhi e cho daor dhuinn,
Ri fraoch an Taoibh-Tuath.

Well get cattle and sheep;
We'll get wheat on the fields, —
And it won't be so dear
As the heath of the north.

'N uair a thèid mi do'n mhunadh,
A mach le mo ghunna,
Cha bhi geamair no duine
'G am chur air an ruaig.

When I go to the mountains,
And roam with my musket,
No keeper, or living,
Will drive me away.

The old inn at Pitmain was demolished about 1860.

Beyond Pitmain, the traveller has a great view of Creag Dhubh, the prominent hill to the west of Newtonmore. "Creag Dhubh" is the traditional the war-cry of the Clan Macpherson. The prevailing wind in Badenoch comes from the west, and whenever the top of Creag Dhubh is shrouded in mist, it is to be expected that a shower of rain - or worse - is on the way.

About a mile beyond Pitmain Farm, an unsurfaced road branches off to the right, gradually climbing the side of the hill. A short distance up this track, but out of sight of the road below, are the ruins of Ballachroan, sometime the home of Captain John Macpherson, commonly known as the Black Officer *(Othaichear Dubh)*. Some say that he had a dark complexion. Others attribute the dark aspect to his presumed association with the devil! The Captain is best known with reference to the circumstances of his death in 1800, and that story can be found in Chapter 7 (Glen Tromie). However, his life was equally fascinating. Born in Glen Truim in 1724, he served for many years in the British army, retiring with the rank of Captain to take up the activity of recruiting officer in his native district. There are many stories of how he took young men unawares, committing them to a lifetime of military service. He also took over the tenancy of Ballachroan, and like his neighbour, John Maclean, he set about improving the standard of husbandry. This he did by adding lime to the peaty soil and spreading sand to make the ground more workable; and the outcome was an abundant crop. He also practised crop rotation and introduced turnips, which were not then widely known. Perhaps it was his outstanding crops which gave rise to the suggestion that he had entered into an arrangement with the Devil. There was indeed the story that he had an agreement with the Devil whereby the Devil would take the roots of whatever the Captain planted. In the first year, the Captain only sowed barley. He harvested his crop; and when the Devil came for his share, the Captain told the Devil that he could take the roots, as agreed in their contract. The Devil was angry at having been so cheated, and insisted that in the following year, he would take the crop and leave the Captain with the roots. Unsurprisingly, the Captain then planted potatoes and turnips; and when the Devil discovered that he was again to get nothing, he departed in a rage - only returning to seal the fate of the Captain in Gaick.

In 1792, when the "new" church was established in Kingussie on its present site, the Captain took the stone from the old church (in the Middle

Ballachroan

Churchyard) for the construction of his new house at Ballachroan - a cardinal sin in the eyes of some.

Passing Ballachroan, the road crosses the Allt Laraidh burn. On the other side of this stream, the former Altlarie Farm has been completely transformed by the creation of the Highland Folk Park, greatly expanding on the Folk Museum which Dr Isabel Grant established in Kingussie. Dr Grant called that Museum "Am Fasgadh" (the Shelter) and it is appropriate that this name has now been given to the new building at the east end of the complex.

Suggested walk

A recently constructed path to the south of Loch Gynack provides a scenic route between Kingussie and Newtonmore. Gynack Road, from the Duke of Gordon Hotel, leads to the Golf Course caravan site. The path begins here, leading through woodland and gradually rising to a point overlooking the Loch. Here turn left on a clear track, and after passing the Loch, the route crosses open country with great views around... eventually following the edge of a plantation. At the end of this woodland, our route turns sharp left, and heads down the Allt Laraidh to the east end of Newtonmore. At the time of writing, a bridge over the Allt Laraidh had been washed away and had not been replaced. The alternative is to cross over to the township of Strone, and follow the surfaced road down to Newtonmore.

Allt Laraidh Falls

Clan Macpherson Museum

Wildcat Trail

Chapter 10
Newtonmore - The Wildcat Village

Newtonmore had its origins early in the 19th century. When an inn was established in 1822 in the white building now known as Craigellachie House (adjacent to the Mains House Care Home) it was described as being in the "Moor of Banchor"; and the township on the site of the Highlander Hotel was known as the Muir of Strone *(Sliabh-na-Strone)*. John Thomson's Atlas of 1832 shows the name "Newton" and it is generally acknowledged that the village as it is now known ("new town on the moor") had its origins about this time.

Newtonmore was on the route taken by many of the drovers; and prior to the opening of the railway in 1863, the level ground below the railway, which now forms the golf course was the location for the annual market. This extended over several days each October and the whole area was taken up with the sale of cattle, sheep, horses and other livestock. However, not only did the railway take the place of the drovers, established markets attached to railway stations like Kingussie caused the downfall of the traditional markets. After the formation of the golf course at Newtonmore, a commentator compared the former activities of the drovers with the then golfers -

"Where there used to be the drovers with their cromags, there are now to be seen human beings in the height of fashion, albeit strangely attired at times, and they also have cromags not so terribly dissimilar in form from those that used to be employed by the drovers as goads for their unruly charges. But those pieces of timber to-day are golf sticks, and it is averred that even from the owners of these and the accompanying unruly balls strange language is sometimes heard - strong even - which plain unsophisticated people declare cannot be distinguished from the swearing of the old time drovers!"

When Queen Victoria travelled west in September 1873, she described Newtonmore as a very poor long village. At that time there were few slated houses in the whole village, and most of the houses presented a most dilapidated appearance. However the opening of the railway in 1863 brought in a major influx of tourists from the south, and in the thirty years that followed, many substantial dwellinghouses were built.

Whereas Kingussie was incorporated as a Burgh with its own Provost and Council, and was thereafter (between 1974 and 1996) the capital of the Council District of Badenoch and Strathspey, Newtonmore was never incorporated and has always had to rely on various voluntary bodies. However, this has generated great enthusiasm for many community activities... including those associated with the Scottish wildcat.

The Scottish wildcat is now only found in the Highlands and is an endangered species with perhaps only a few hundred remaining in the wild. The author can testify that the cat is still in Badenoch. Because of its very limited numbers and its nocturnal habits, it is rarely seen. Larger than the domestic cat, a particular feature is its thick tail, ringed with bands of black and brown, and ending with a blunt black tip. Traditionally, the wildcat has been regarded as Scotland's most ferocious animal; and even when brought up in a domestic environment, it has never been tamed.

The wildcat is associated with several Scottish Clans, including the Clan Macpherson which has its heartlands in Badenoch. Indeed, within the heraldic arms of the Chief of the Clan Macpherson first recorded in 1672, is "Crest a cat sejant [sitting] proper"; and various images of a wildcat appear in the arms of other Macphersons. Also the motto "Touch not the cat bot a glove" (Touch not the cat when it is without a glove), reflects the ferocious nature of the wildcat.

It is therefore not surprising that the community of Newtonmore has adopted the wildcat. The orbital path round Newtonmore is known as the Wildcat Trail; and when the Information Bureau was opened in the Main Street, it was appropriately headed "The Wildcat Centre". Inspired by the model cows which appeared in various cities around the world, Newtonmore arranged for some life-size wildcats to be individually painted and these can be found in gardens, on roofs and in windows throughout the village. There are now about 130 cats, and it is an open challenge to find all of them.

Coming from Kingussie, the Highland Folk Museum is the traveller's first introduction to Newtonmore. Although the Museum was only recently moved and expanded within its present site, it has a history going back some 40 years.

Dr Isabel Grant (who is also referred to in Chapter 2) was born in Edinburgh in 1887. A distant ancestor was William Mackintosh of Balnespick who had farmed at Dunachton in the 18th century; and her first book was based on the account books of that farm. On her travels through Europe, Dr Grant, was greatly influenced by the open air museum movement, and in particular, the "Skansen" in Stockholm, Sweden, and by the "Maihaugen", in Lillehammer, Norway. There she saw "activities" and not just "objects" being preserved. Dr Grant resolved to record as much as she could of the long-established ways of Highland life which were quickly disappearing, and to preserve many of the associated objects. She bought a disused church on the island of Iona in 1935 to accommodate her growing collection. She called her museum Am Fasgadh ("The Shelter") because "it was to shelter homely ancient things from destruction". Within three years the Iona building was found to be too small; and in 1939 Dr Grant moved her museum to Laggan. Five years later, Dr Grant moved again, this time to the former Pitmain Lodge, at the corner of Duke Street and Spey Street in Kingussie. She made full use of outbuildings to display larger items; and within the grounds of the Lodge, she commissioned the building of several traditional houses. This was the days of steam trains, and sadly sparks from these trains ignited the grass on an embankment, and then the heather thatch on one of those buildings. Upon Dr Grant's retirement in 1954, the Museum was managed by a University Trust; then in 1975, the Museum was taken over by Highland Council. Dr Grant maintained an active interest in the Museum until her death in 1983 at the age of 96. More recently Highland Council acquired Altlaurie Farm and have developed the present "Highland Folk Museum" on multiple sites over an extended area, perhaps fulfilling Dr Grant's ultimate dream. Significantly, the most recent building has been named "Am Fasgadh" in her memory.

Behind the reception box, and close to the railway, there is a small mound. The first (six inch) Ordnance Survey map of 1870 shows that here was the remains of a Stone Circle known as Tom a' Chladha, that stone cists, urns and human remains were found at this site in 1860, and that silver coins were found nearby in 1866. There are now no obvious signs of a stone circle, but there is a depression indicative of a small archeological excavation. The present location of the relics is not known.

The Balavil Hotel has a prominent position in Newtonmore and its name might appear surprising, considering that Balavil House and Estate are on the other side of Kingussie. The explanation is that shortly after James Macpherson, the "translator" of Ossian, purchased the Estate of Raitts in 1788 and renamed it "Belleville" (later to become "Balavil"), he also acquired the lands of Clune, Strone and Banchor (around the present Newtonmore). In 1890, the inn on this site was appropriately known as the Belleville Arms Hotel and early into the 20th century, when the hotel was developed, the new name was adopted. After the Second World War, the hotel was acquired by Ewen Ormiston, who had sporting interests in the district. He recognised the tourist potential of the "garron" ponies that were used to take deer carcasses from the hills, and began the new activity of pony-trekking.

Opposite the War Memorial and the Village Hall, the Glen Road branches off to the right. Before the first bend in the road, the stone clad St Bride's Church has a prominent site on the right.

Ecclesiastically, Newtonmore is in the Parish of Kingussie. In 1894, it was recognised that the population of Newtonmore which had increased to about 600, warranted a separate place of worship; and a mission church (St Columba's) was established in Station Road, near to the junction with Laggan Road. Around the same time, the United Free Church of Scotland built their own church (St Andrew's) in the centre of Newtonmore. Although the Churches amalgamated in 1929, separate services continued until 1955. St Columba's was demolished and the stone was used to reshape St Andrew's – and in 1958, the new church was opened – adopting the name St Bride's – a name historically linked with the immediate area. In Station Road, a dwellinghouse fronted by the original railings, now occupies the site of the former St Columba's Church.

Water supply is essential for a community and on the left side of the Glen Road, a small gate leads down to the Well of the Alder *(Fuaran lag an Dromain* - the spring of the hollow of the ridge). A sign adjacent to the Well relates that when Christianity was introduced to the Highlands by Irish misionaries in the 6th century, wells were brought into the new belief system as "holy wells". The Irish saint most clearly associated with the cult of holy wells was St Bridget - better known in Scotland as St Bride, a name which is very familiar to Newtonmore. The notice also tells us that "Brigit" was a Celtic goddess and that her wells were associated with healing, with fortune telling, and with fertility. Long after a piped water supply was introduced

Glen Banchor

River Calder

into Newtonmore, villagers continued to draw this water because of its apparent purity.

Strategically placed where the roads to Perth and Laggan divide, stands the Clan Macpherson Museum. The Museum was established in 1952 to display the relics from Cluny Castle which had been purchased in public auction. Supported solely by donations, the Museum welcomes visitors from April to October seven days a week.

The Laggan Road takes us to a signpost in Gaelic pointing the way to St Bride's burial ground *(Cladh Brighde)*, otherwise known as Banchor Cemetery. For many centuries it was used for those who had lived around the present Newtonmore. The cemetery also served former residents from the other side of the Spey. Prior to the first bridge being built in 1765, there was a ferry - downstream of the present bridge; and a "coffin road" followed a direct route under the railway. In 1875, the tenant of Banchor Farm barricaded the way to the cemetery and began to build a farm steading across the road. This brought an inevitable storm of protest which was ignored. An action was raised in the Court of Session in Edinburgh by Peter Cattanach, a lawyer who had local connections, seeking to renew the access road to the cemetery. The outcome was that a new road was constructed; and to ensure that no future encroachment should he made upon legal rights, a public notice was erected. This notice read;

An Rathad Daingnichte Le Lach.
Gu Cladh Brighde -

BANCHOR CEMETERY

(The Roadway Established by Law. To St Bride's Graveyard)

On 30 June 2014, a replacement sign, with the same inscription, was dedicated in a memorable ceremony. Banchor Cemetery is relatively new, but it is believed that the site of the original 6th century chapel is within the present graveyard.

It might be added that R L Stevenson walked from Kingussie on two occasions and visited Banchor Cemetery, where he became intrigued by a gravestone, bearing a Gaelic inscription in memory of Catriona Kennedy, and

Banchor Cemetery

that this inspired him to adopt the name "Catriona" as the title for a subsequent novel.

Suggested walk

As already mentioned in this Chapter, the orbital path round Newtonmore is known as "The Wildcat Trail". It extends for seven miles - from the banks of the Spey to the moorland above the village and is clearly signposted throughout with the symbol of a cat. Because the route crosses the public road at either end of the village, it is possible to limit an outing to one half of the trail - leaving the second half to another day.

Chapter 11
Newtonmore to Laggan

The road to Laggan branches off to the right of the Clan Macpherson Museum and leaves Newtonmore at the bridge over the River Calder. The original bridge was constructed by Thomas Telford in 1814 but was badly damaged in a flood in 1978. A plaque on the north parapet records that the present replacement bridge was completed in 1982.

On the west bank of the Calder is Biallid House, one of the historic houses of the Clan Macpherson. In the adjoining stable there was the Newtonmore Riding Centre - now re-established in Kingussie. Reference has been made in Chapter 10 to Ewen Ormiston recognising that the garron ponies which were kept for deer stalking might also be used for recreational riding; and it is this interest in horses that is continued by Ewen's grandson at the Centre.

On the right of the road about a mile beyond the Calder bridge, is an old burial ground known to some as Cladh Phadruig (St Patrick's Burial Ground) and to others as Cladh Pheadail (the Burial Ground of St Peter). Most of the headstones bear Macpherson names. There are also a few McIntyres. It is believed that there was at one time a chapel here, and that the prehistoric parish included the whole of Glen Truim and the valley of Loch Ericht.

About a half mile beyond the burial ground, and immediately before a plantation on the right, there is an unmarked area of six acres which was gifted in 1939, to named trustees for the Clan Macpherson. In 1949, those trustees transferred ownership of the ground to the Clan Macpherson Association.

Across from the plantation, one comes upon two small lochs in the flood plain of the Spey. These lochs, known collectively as Loch-an Ovie (or as it appears in Ordnance Survey maps - Lochain Uvie), the name apparently derived from *ubhaidh* meaning "dreadful" or "awe inspiring". In 1926, DH Lawrence spent some time in Newtonmore, and on 12 August of that year, he sent to a friend a post card of Loch-an Ovie with the following comment -

"...I was never in the Highlands before - find it rather attractive, though a bit cold and showery. Today grouse-shooting begins, but of course I'm not one

Map 6

Suggested walks — — —

miles
0 1 2

Tromie Bridge
B970
Ruthven
Lynaberack
Glen Tromie
Gaick
River Spey
A9
Ralia
Phoines
Loch Cuaich
Newtonmore
A86
Cluny's Cave
Glentruim House
Etteridge
A9
Glen Banchor
Loch-an Ovie
Craigdhu House
Cluny's Cairn
Cruban Beag
Falls of Truim
Presmuchrach
Monadhliaths
Cluny Castle
River Spey
Breakachy
Raeburn Hut
Crubenmore
River Truim
A9
River Calder
Balgowan
A86
Drumgask
Catlodge
A889
Loch Caoldair
Laggan Bridge
Dalchully
A86
Dalwhinnie
102

to go banging at the birds. The heather is just out - bell-heather dying - and the harebells are lovely. The motor-cars spoil it all, though – they never cease passing on these narrow little roads. We motor to the various lakes, and picnic, making fires with very damp wood. Which is my news..."

Nothing has changed !

Looking ahead on the top of the nearest hill (Creag Bheag Uvie), is a monument to Sarah Justina Davidson, who died on 14 March 1886. She was the widow of Ewen Macpherson ("Old Cluny") who succeeded as Chief of the Clan Macpherson in 1817, and who died in 1885. The monument is a replica of a larger monument to her late husband which can be seen from further along the road. Towering above Loch-an Ovie are the cliffs of Creag Dhubh. To members of the Clan Macpherson, the cave high up on these cliffs is a symbol of the nine years, after the battle of Culloden (1746), which Ewen Macpherson of Cluny ("Cluny of the '45") spent in hiding. We are told that the cave was dug by clansmen during the night and that the excavated material was deposited in Loch-an-Ovie. It is said that the original cave was some twenty-five or thirty feet in length and four or five feet wide, with sufficient height for a medium-sized man to stand upright. Deep fissures in the rocky wall of the cave were cunningly converted into loopholes which provided a very convenient means of observing the surrounding country. If the cave was to have been discovered, it would only have been by chance or through treachery. Even if a fire was kindled, the smoke would have blended so well with the weather-beaten rock that it would have been impossible to detect. Although it is not immediately evident, it is said that the original cave has partially collapsed; as what now exists would be too confined to accommodate more than one or two persons for any length of time. The present cave is narrow throughout its length and runs parallel to the side of the cliff in an easterly direction. In its principal part it is some twenty feet long and it varies between five and six feet in height. It is thus possible to walk into the cave without much stooping. The floor is mainly of hard-packed earth, but there are a few outcrops of rock which would make the cave uncomfortable to sleep in. The width of the floor is in places no more than a foot, but it widens at waist level to some three or four feet and narrows again towards the roof. The walls are too uneven to give any accurate measurements, particularly near roof level where there is a sloping shelf in places. At the far end of the cave is a small compartment at a slightly higher

Creag Dubh - location of Cluny's Cave

St. Ternan's Cemetery

level, and this might have been used as a fireplace or store. It is only about four feet high and five feet long, and has a rough and rocky floor. A feature of this small compartment is its two small openings, one on the roof and the other in a corner of the floor, which not only give some light to the cave but also keep it dry and aired. There is a similar opening in the principal part of the cave. No signs of any former occupation can be seen, but Grant R. Francis in his *Romance of the White Rose* (1933) tells of a sgian dubh and a small drinking cup having been found in the cave. The entrance to the cave is concealed by a huge ledge of rock, which would completely mislead any stranger. The rock also forms the doorstep to the cave, for every visitor must step on this rock before jumping down into the mouth of the cave. There are now only one or two trees in the close vicinity and, in contrast to former days, anyone entering or leaving the cave can easily be seen from the road below. There is a tradition that the hillside was heavily wooded in the eighteenth century, and this must have been so because the Hanoverian Forces under Sir Hector Munro never found the cave.

For anyone staying in Badenoch or passing through the district, a visit to the cave on Creag Dhubh makes a most interesting afternoon; and from the mouth of the cave, there are magnificent views down to Loch-an Ovie and over Glen Truim and as far as the Cairngorm plateau. A herd of feral goats can sometimes be observed, leaping from rock to rock. However, any expedition should not be taken lightly as it entails a hard and steep climb, the ground can be very slippery, and the final approach is very exposed. For these reasons any intending visitor should be accompanied by someone who is already familiar with the route.

Cluny had other hiding-places, most of them artificial, which he occupied during his nine years in Badenoch, after Culloden. The best known of his artificial structures was the famous "Cage" in the vicinity of Ben Alder, where Cluny entertained Prince Charles Edward Stuart in September 1746. Another hideout was dug into the hillside on the other side of the Spey opposite Loch-an Ovie. Between 1746 and 1755, Cluny's continued residence in Badenoch was regarded by the Hanoverian Government as constituting a major security risk, and there was a reward of one thousand guineas (£1050) for information leading to his capture. Accordingly he never remained long in any one place and, if his presence became known to more than one family, he had to move on. Very few of his hiding places were ever discovered by his enemies.

Immediately beyond Loch-an Ovie is Craigdhu House. The original building was constructed by Old Cluny for his mother. On her death, Old Cluny gave the property to his daughter Caroline Catherine who had married George Dartmouth Fitzroy, a naval captain. George Fitzroy was a distant relative of Robert Fitzroy, who commanded HMS Beagle which took Charles Darwin to the Galapagos.

After passing Craigdhu House, the valley of the Spey opens out; and on the top of a distant hill can be seen the monument to Old Cluny. Immediately after a narrow bridge, there is a gateway leading to Cluny Castle. It was around here that that there was the first change of horses on the coach from Kingussie to Tulloch.

In his *A Day's March to Ruin* (1996), Alan G Macpherson tells the story of Cluny of the '45. A month before Prince Charles Edward Stuart landed at Loch nam Uamh on 25 July 1745, Cluny had accepted a Commission as Captain in the Earl of Loudon's (Hanoverian) regiment. As the Prince came over the Corrieyairack Pass, the Jacobites understandably had doubts about Cluny's loyalty. On the evening of Wednesday 28 August, Cluny House (as it was then known) was surrounded by a detachment of Camerons, and Cluny was taken into custody. On the following day, the whole party set off, catching up with the Prince at Dalwhinnie. The Prince persuaded Cluny to change his allegiance; and Cluny briefly returned home to recruit his clansmen to the Jacobite cause.

The present Cluny Castle occupies a prominent site overlooking the Spey valley and the property can be clearly seen from the road. The previous building was destroyed by the Hanoverian troops in June 1746. As previously mentioned in this Chapter, Cluny of the '45 was a fugitive for nine years, before escaping to France.

On Christmas Day 1754, the young Ensign Hector Munro and a party of Hanoverian soldiers surrounded the house where Cluny was living. There being no means of escape, Cluny went into the kitchen, where a servant man was sitting and exchanged clothes with him; and when Munro rode up to the door, Cluny ran out and held the stirrup while the officer was dismounting. Cluny walked the horse about while Munro was in the house, and when he came out again, Cluny again held the stirrup for him to mount. At this point, he was asked by the officer if he knew where Cluny was... to which he answered that he did not, and that if he did, he would not tell him. Munro is said to have replied - "I believe you would not; you are a good fellow, here is a shilling for you". It is this scene which is replicated in a magnificent silver epergne (or candelabrum) which was presented to Cluny's grandson ("Old Cluny") and his wife Sarah on the occasion of their golden wedding in 1882. The silver candelabrum can now be seen in the Clan Macpherson Museum in Newtonmore.

There is another version of the story, related by Alexander Mackenzie in his History of the Munros, that the young Ensign knew Cluny quite well, and that he actually winked at him as he threw him the coin! Thereafter, Munro had an outstanding military career in India and finally retired from the army in 1798 with the rank of full General.

Cluny's only son was born in a corn-kiln where his mother was sheltering, and in consequence, he was ever after described as "Duncan of the Kiln". Notwithstanding his background, Duncan was commissioned as an officer in the British Army, and saw active service during the American War of Independence. Latterly the Forfeited Estate Commissioners granted Duncan a lease of the Cluny Estates, and they were eventually restored to him in 1784. Soon after, Duncan built the present house which has since become known as Cluny Castle.

Duncan's son, Ewen, was respectfully known as "Old Cluny". He was Chief of the Clan from 1817 to his death in 1885; and this was undoubtably a memorable period in the history of the Clan. Indeed, the following description appeared in *The Celtic Magazine* of April 1878 -

"High up in Badenoch, nine miles from Kingussie, on a slight eminence on the right of the road leading to Fort-William, stands Cluny Castle, the residence of Cluny Macpherson of Cluny, Chief of Clan Chattan. It is a plain but substantial building, commanding a magnificent prospect. The situation and its surroundings are just such as a great Highland Chief would be expected to choose for his home - retired, yet, for the district, central; the country subdued, open, and fertile in the immediate vicinity; but in the distance, on all sides, bold, majestic, grand, the Grampian range and the Cairngorms standing out in their magnificent 'snow-capped towers,' and forming a prominent and awe-inspiring scene. The furnishings - warlike instruments, illustrative of the past: targets, battle-axes, claymores, swords, dirks, guns, pistols, old armour, banners, stag and rams' heads, wild cats, swans, foreign heads and birds, and numberless other trophies of the battle and the chase - old relics and curiosities - evidence the taste of its occupant and the warlike predilections of the old cavalier race from which he sprang.

The old Chief himself - a well-knit, erect, sturdy Highlander, about the middle height, dressed in full Highland costume - salutes you in the Gaelic vernacular of his ancestors, which he speaks with purity and ease. He begins to show signs of advancing years, but still looking twenty years younger than he really is. The natural affability and courteous ease of manner characteristic of him, in spite of an unconscious air of dignity of countenance and of motion, at once puts his visitor at perfect ease, who soon finds himself discoursing on old Highland feuds and clan battles which naturally lead up to the doings and history of the Risings of the Fifteen and the Forty-five, in which his ancestors had taken such a prominent but unfortunate part.

The present Chief, Cluny Macpherson of Cluny, is one of the few genuine remaining links that connect the "good old days" of the patriarchal chiefs, who cherished and were proud of their people, and the present, when generally the lairds look upon the ancient inhabitants of the soil much the same way as a cattle-dealer looks upon his herd to make the most of them. The House of Cluny has a history and a genuine respect among the Highlanders of which he may well be, and is, justly proud; for the family have always taken a distinguished share in everything calculated to advance the interests of the country."

The reference to "Clan Chattan" requires some explanation. Clan Chattan was a confederation of a number of clans, also including the Mackintoshes, Shaws, Macgillivrays, Davidsons, and Farquharsons – by tradition, all having been descended from a single ancestor. Throughout the centuries, the Macphersons and the Mackintoshes maintained competing claims to being Chief of Clan Chattan and hence the designation in the foregoing passage.

When Old Cluny died in 1885, he was succeeded as chief of the Clan and Laird of Cluny by his eldest son, Duncan who died in the following year. Old Cluny's second son, Colonel Ewen (Henry Davidson) then succeeded.

Andrew Carnegie was born in Dunfermline in 1835, and left that town as a youth when his parents emigrated in 1848. He lived his early life in and around Pittsburg, and he only moved to New York when he had become one of the richest men in the iron and steel industry. However, at an early stage, he developed an interest in travel, coming over to Europe each Summer and invariably visiting his native Dunfermline.

Carnegie did not marry until 1887, and in that year he took the lease of Kilgraston House, situated on the hill between Perth and Bridge of Earn. Louise, his new wife, had heard the bagpipes being played in Edinburgh and begged that there should be piper at their new Scottish home – who might walk round and waken them in the morning and also to play them in to dinner. In his autobiography, Carnegie observed that although his wife was American to the core, and a Connecticut Puritan at that, she had declared that if she were condemned to live upon a lonely island and allowed to choose only one musical instrument, it would be the pipes. There was great response to Carnegie's advertisement, but he was particularly drawn to a John Macpherson of Laggan. John Macpherson was still a young man, but he had an outstanding backgound. His grandfather had learned his piping skills from the last of the MacCrimmons of Skye; and his father was Malcolm Macpherson, "Calum Piobair", who had been piper to Old Cluny. John presented his credentials from the then Cluny (Ewen Macpherson); and Carnegie is reputed to have said "What is good enough for Cluny Macpherson is surely good enough for Andrew Carnegie".

John Macpherson was duly appointed and proceeded to Kilgraston House to welcome the Carnegies to their first home in Scotland. Mr and Mrs Carnegie took John Macpherson back with them to New York at the end of the Summer. Andrew Carnegie relates in his autobiography that it was Louise, his wife, who wanted a wilder and more Highland home, and in the following year (1888) when the Carnegies were offered the lease of Cluny Castle, it was John Macpherson who influenced them in their selection of that residence. (Colonel Ewen welcomed the opportunity of a summer let of the Castle: he was still involved in his military career, and unmarried, and two recent deaths in successive years had no doubt put financial pressure on the Cluny Estates).

From the beginning, Andrew Carnegie hosted large house parties; he particularly enjoyed fishing and hunting, and he had the run of the whole of the eleven thousand acres of Cluny Estate. Such was the pleasure of Cluny Castle that Andrew Carnegie funded the building of the present west wing – to accommodate a billiard room. The Carnegies came to Cluny Castle for ten successive years, and indeed they would have bought the whole Estate. However, by this time, Ewen had retired from his army duties and had just married (at the age of 60). He was not willing to sell the ancestral home at any price, and this caused the Carnegies to acquire and develop Skibo Castle, in Sutherland.

Colonel Ewen died 1900. Old Cluny's third son, George Gordon Macpherson, had died in 1891, and on the death of Colonel Ewen, his heir male and therefore his successor as Clan Chief was George Gordon's surviving son Ewen George, then nine years of age. Ewen George emigrated to Australia at an early age; and died in 1965. He was succeeded by Francis Cameron, a great grandson of Duncan of the Kiln, who died later that same year. The present Chief is a descendant of an uncle of Cluny of the '45.

It should be explained that Old Cluny's third son, George Gordon Macpherson had disgraced himself financially and had been disinherited. Accordingly when Colonel Ewen died in 1900, the Estate of Cluny was inherited – not by George Gordon's son – but by Old Cluny's youngest son Albert Cameron Macpherson. In acknowledging that his nephew was the true chief, Albert Cameron was merely known as "of Cluny". When Albert Cameron died in 1932, Cluny Estate was bankrupt; and in 1943, the remaining Cluny lands were sold. The ancient relics were sold by auction, and it was fortunate that many of them were bought by enthusiastic members of the Clan, who then established the Museum in 1952 at its present site in Newtonmore.

Close to the roadway, inset into the grounds of Cluny Castle, is St. Ternan's Cemetery (Cladh Chluanaidh or Cladh Tornan), the burial ground of the Chiefs and other members of the Cluny Macpherson family. However, it was never a private graveyard - as it will be seen from the headstones that many of those buried came from outwith the Cluny Estate. There is no adjacent parking, and any visitor to this graveyard is advised to park at the west gate of Cluny, and carefully walk the few yards back.

On the right of the road, about a mile beyond Cluny, is the stock farm of Gaskbeg. The farm-house was at one time the manse for Laggan Parish, and as such, occupied by the husband of Mrs Anne Grant, whose *Letters from the Mountains and Tales of the Highlands* made her name well known in the literary world. Born Anne Macvicar in Glasgow in 1755, her early years were in New York State and Vermont prior to the American Revolution. Latterly her father was barrack master at Fort Augustus. Anne remembered, when she was 18, Dr Samuel Johnston and James Boswell visiting the Fort as part of their tour in 1773. The Rev James Grant was chaplain at the Fort for two years until 1775, when he became parish minister at Laggan. Anne and James were married in 1779, and they lived in a small cottage for some years until the substantial manse was built. After she was widowed in 1801, Anne moved, latterly to Edinburgh, dying there in 1838.

Further along the road, occupying a prominent position, is the Parish Church of Laggan. The present church was built by Duncan of the Kiln in 1785 shortly after the Cluny Estate was restored to him. It replaced a simple building some distance upstream, near Blaragie. The Church was practically rebuilt in 1806 after a fire and again in 1842. A particular feature is the high pulpit. The pew in the middle of the gallery was for members of the Cluny family, and the pulpit was intended to be at a height such that the minister did not have to look up or down when addressing the laird. However, it is now recognised that the pulpit is rather remote from the congregation, and it is therefore rarely used.

Since the 1980s, Laggan and Newtonmore have shared the same minister.

Leaving the Church, the main road turns sharp left to cross the Spey, and a branch road on the right leads to the Corrieyairick - each road taking us to subsequent chapters in this book.

Suggested walk

In the previous Chapter (Chapter 10), there is reference to the Gaelic signpost on the Laggan Road pointing the way to Banchor Cemetery. To the left of this road is a gate which takes one on to the path which leads upstream above the River Calder. This is a particularly scenic route set into the hillside, with the river struggling through a narrow defile below. The path eventually comes out into the open and comes up to join the Glen Banchor road. The public road ends immediately before a bridge over the Allt a' Chaorainn, but it is possible to walk on, following a good track as Glen Banchor stretches on between Craig Dhu and the Monadhliaths. To return, stay on the Glen Road all the way down to Newtonmore.

Laggan Parish Church

It is possible to continue to the head of Glen Banchor and then turn left on a good track which leads down to the Laggan Road at Cluny Mains This route has been incorporated into the East Highland Way and a detailed description can be found in the Walk Highlands website. The distance from Newtonmore via Glen Banchor to Cluny Mains is about eight miles, and might take about four hours; but it should be added that at the head of Glen Banchor, there are two streams which may be difficult to cross after heavy rain.

Wade Road near Dalchully

Chapter 12
Laggan to the Corrieyairack

The Corrieyairack pass from Fort Augustus into the upper Spey was a traditional drove road; and indeed droving continued over this route until the end of the 19th century.

General Wade recognised the potential and in 1731, he built his new road from Dalwhinnie to Fort Augustus in order to provide a direct connection from the south to the Great Glen – where there was a line of forts from Fort William to Inverness (Fort George). Crossing the Monadhliaths at 2500 feet, the Corrieyairack is the highest road ever constructed in Britain. The most difficult part of the road was in the corrie on the east side of the summit, which gives the pass its name. Here the road overcame a particularly steep slope with some 18 zigzags, later reduced to about 13.

An early traveller was Mrs Anne Grant of Laggan (referred to in Chapter 11). She recorded that eleven soldiers perished on the hill over the first winter after the road had been built. On returning to Fort Augustus in 1781 for a family visit she writes -

"You will think I am talking very solemnly about travelling the twenty-five miles between here and Laggan; for I do not know that ever I told you how peculiarly we are situated with regard to each other. This district is divided from ours by an immense mountain called Corryarrick. That barrier is impassable in the depth of winter, as the top of it is above the region of clouds; and the sudden descent on the other side peculiarly dangerous, not only from deep snows concealing the unbeaten track of the road, but from whirlwinds and eddies that drive the snow into heaps; besides an evil spirit which the country people devoutly believe to have dwelt there time out of mind."

Anne Grant does not indicate her method of travelling. Lord Cockburn, who was a Court of Session judge between 1834 and his death in 1854, recorded that his first visit into the Highlands was in 1798, when "with two other boys, I made a tour in a gig to Inverness, and home by Fort Augustus, and over Corryarrick". J B Salmond, in his *Wade in Scotland* has an extended description of the Hon Mrs Murray crossing in the same year -.

"At the commencement of the zigzag, I got out of the carriage and walked down at my leisure; amusing myself by picking up curious stones and pebbles in the channels made by the torrents, which cross the road at every five or ten yards. Round the base of the mountain, at some distance from the zigzag, is a stream, into which the other torrents dash; leaving behind them broad channels of smooth round stones, washed from higher parts. The road is so cut up by these violent torrents from the top of the zigzag to the entrance on the plain, that for four or five miles scarcely ten yards can be found free of them: which is indeed sufficient to pull a slight carriage to pieces. Allen led the horses, and the wheels being dragged, he came quietly and safely to the bottom of that extraordinary pass..."

As noted by Mrs Grant, the Corrieyairack was notorious because of its winter snowstorms, the Hon Mrs Murray observing that soldiers had often perished by imprudently drinking quantities of spirits, thinking thereby to keep out the cold; but alas! It was the sure way to destruction. Salmond also describes a journey undertaken by the local Catholic priest on 27 December 1819 -

"The good father had taken with him on this occasion four men and a pony. So deep was the snow that they lost their way. They left it to the pony to find the road, the men following behind in single file, each holding on to the other, and the foremost to the pony's tail. So they came safely to their destination."

It is not surprising that by about 1830, the road over the pass ceased to be in general use.

By the 20th century, the road had grassed over and it had become an established recreational route. However, with the development of the internal combustion engine, it also became recognised by the respective Estates that the road provided easy access to the higher parts; and further traffic came with the introduction of electricity pylons over the pass. More recently, the road has been "discovered" by the owners of 4 x 4 vehicles as the ultimate challenge, and understandably there has since been a campaign to discourage all but essential vehicular traffic.

Ironically, the first hostile troop movement on the Corrieyairack was in August 1745 when about 3000 Jacobites with Prince Charles Edward Stuart at their head, crossed from west to east. Sir John Cope, with an inexperienced and ill-equiped force of some 1400 Hanoverian troops had been sent north from Crieff to confront the Highlanders. Cope, no doubt fearing what ultimately happened to him at Prestonpans, turned away to Ruthven and on to Inverness – leaving the road south open to the Highlanders, who were then able to proceed to Edinburgh without resistance.

The present-day motorist can drive eleven miles from Laggan to Melgarve, leaving only four miles to the summit of the pass. We begin opposite the Parish Church (at the village shop), where we branch right. This is not General Wade's route, but it is now the only motor road which follows the Spey upstream from this point.

It may be noticed that many of the townships around Laggan have the prefix or suffix "gask" - a gask being a small hill consisting of glacial debris. As an early example, we pass Gergask School – Glenbogle School of the "Monarch of the Glen" television series.

We pass Blaragie Farm. A famous "son" of Blaragie was John Macpherson. He acted as orderly sergeant to General Wolfe at the Battle of Quebec (1759), and had the distinguished honour of receiving the dying hero into his arms, when he fell mortally wounded. Soon after, a commission was conferred on John Macpherson. Like most Highland officers, he retired on half-pay, and turned his attention to farming; and eventually died in 1815 aged 88 years.

Beyond Blaragie farm, the road bears left down to the Spey; and after a further half mile, an access road on the right leads up to Coul. At the far side of a field to the right of this access road, there are some remains of what may have been a Druidical Circle – some 64 feet in diameter (NN 590 940). It has been suggested that this may have been a burial ground, but there is no sign of any gravestones.

Continuing along the road for a further half mile, in a field to the right, there is perhaps a more interesting relic (NN 587 937). Although close to the road, it is preferable to go through one of the gates at the end of the field to gain access. This was the site of the original Catholic chapel of St Michael, probably built about 1803, as there is a record of the Catholic population of the district prior to this date, walking to Sunday Mass at Roy Bridge via Glen Roy – the distance being such that they had to leave on the Saturday evening! The chapel at Coul was superseded in 1845 by a chapel to be built on the other side of the Spey – which we come to later in our journey. Within a stone circle, there is a single heavily carved standing stone. About one metre in height, the stone appears to have been the lower part of the shaft of a stone cross. The carvings have been described as follows -

"One side (facing roughly NE) is carved in relief, clearly showing in the lower half two beasts facing each other, with three-fold snouts nearly touching, upright, with their legs also pointing towards each other. Their ears and eyes are also visible."

The other side (facing roughly SW) appears to have been carved with a cross, with a saltire at the bottom and a strangely asymmetrical lower shaft with possible horizontal marking on the SE side.

The other sides are also carved, with saltires, and at the bottom of the NW side, three small smooth hemispherical bosses are clustered together in a group about 13cm across.

The surveyors who compiled the first Ordnance Survey map of the area recorded that there had been no burials at this site since about 1860.

The surroundings here are dominated by the dam over the Spey, but before coming to this, mention should be made of Crathie – situated to the north of the dam and to the east of the river Markie. In 1841, more than 30 families lived in this village and the adjoining community of Balmishaig – mostly of the Catholic faith. However, the isolation of the area and the effect of two world wars, caused a steady diminution of the population, and the last permanent resident left in 1951. All that is now left is the ruins of the various houses – sad to reflect that this was once a vibrant community.

About a mile up the Markie, there is the old burial ground of Reballich. In *Laggan – Past and Present* (1990), Dr Richardson related that this place was used for unbaptised children and those born out of wedlock; and that the inhabitants of Crathie might curse someone with the expression "may you go to Reballich". The burial ground was in danger of becoming totally overgrown; and a cairn, about five feet in height, was recently erected to ensure that the burial ground is not forgotten. The inscription on the cairn reads "Here lie God's holy and beloved innocents" with the words repeated in Gaelic.

The dam itself is 900 feet in length and 30 feet high; and was engineered to augment the water supply powering the aluminium smelter at Fort William, but was so designed to ensure that an adequate flow of water would always flow down the Spey. The dam was completed in 1943 and the concrete bridge over the Spey dates from this time.

As one climbs up beyond the bridge, there can be seen the line of General Wade's road on the south side of the Spey. Cresting the hill, a rough vehicle track leads upwards for a few yards to a level area and six mature yew trees – all that is left of the Catholic chapel - also named St Michael's Chapel - which was built about 1845 to replace the former building at Coul. It is said to have been of an attractive granite construction with a slate roof, and that it could seat a congregation of over 200. However, as the population moved away, the congregation diminished. A new Catholic church was established in Kingussie in 1932; and Augustus Muir, writing in 1934, noted that the chapel here at Laggan was no longer being used. Sadly, the building then became derelict, and was blown up around 1955 because it had become so dangerous. However, the stone and slates were salvaged and used in the rebuilding of the Priory (now the Abbey) of Pluscarden in Moray. Exceptionally, one dressed granite stone can still be found between the yew trees.

The stretch of water behind the dam extends for about a mile upstream. Strangely, no name was ever given to this new loch, and it is merely known locally as "Spey Dam". At the western end, the water is channeled into a canal leading to Loch Crunachdan in Glen Shirra; and a tunnel then takes the water from the loch down to Loch Laggan. A concrete bridge, similar to the bridge below the dam, takes our road over the canal. Immediately before this bridge, there is a particularly odd sight on the right – a "dry" bridge with an absence of any watercourse: the explanation being that the bridge was built by General Wade to take his road across the stream flowing out of Loch Crunachdan, and that this stream ceased to flow when the tunnel was constructed in 1943. Some say that this was about the furthest point reached by General Cope's army in August 1745, before turning and heading for Ruthven and Inverness. The topic is covered more fully in Chapter 14.

It should perhaps be mentioned that British Aluminium acquired the whole catchment area of the upper Spey when the Spey Dam and the associated works were being constructed, and all these lands are now owned by its successor, Rio Tinto Alcan, and managed as a private estate.

About one and a half miles further, we come to Garvamore, where a long two storey building backs on to the road. Built about 1740 – probably by General Wade - this building has had a multitude of uses. It is likely to have been constructed as an inn or as a "King's House" (such as are still known at Balquhidder and at the head of Glencoe) to accommodate travellers.

Troops were also billeted here and this may be the explanation for the property becoming known as Garvamore Barracks. After the Corrieyairack ceased to be used as a "through road", the building was used as a school and thereafter as family accommodation. For some time it has been largely derelict, although some restoration has been carried out by the owners.

Half a mile beyond the Barracks, we come to a substantial two arch bridge, with prominent buttresses. General Wade completed this crossing of the Spey in 1732 and called it "St George's Bridge", but this name has never come into general use. It is one of Wade's three great bridges; the others being at Aberfeldy – over the Tay, and at Highbridge – downstream from Spean Bridge. Sadly both arches of this last mentioned bridge collapsed many years ago, leaving two enormous pillars rising up from the gorge.

The decision to build St George's Bridge – as we may call it - demonstrates the importance that was given to the building of the road over the Corrieyairack. In contrast, Wade never built any bridges over the rivers Dulnain, Findhorn and Nairn – leaving his troops to ford these rivers, and also the Spey itself, on a journey from Ruthven to Inverness.

Beyond the bridge at Garvamore, there are a further four miles of motorable road up to Melgarve. The cottage here is no longer occupied, but was at one time perhaps the most remote dwellinghouse in Badenoch. About half a mile before Melgarve, there is a small stone, about two feet high, midway between the road and the Spey. This is Cathal's Stone. The origin of the stone is not known, but it is associated with a story that a young Irishman of that name eloped with a daughter of the then Macpherson of Cluny; and that it was here that a search party caught up with the couple and murdered the Irishman before bringing back the girl. It has also been suggested that this stone marks the location of the Battle of Garva (1187).

Also in the vicinity of Melgarve, there are two small Wade bridges, one of which has been replaced by a wooden structure. Beyond Melgarve, one track, very boggy in places, goes straight on and eventually passes the diminutive Loch Spey, the source of the mighty river. After the Loch, there is a very indistinct watershed leading into Glen Roy. Significantly, the watershed is at a height of 1151 feet above sea level, the same height as the uppermost "parallel road" of Glen Roy – the explanation being that towards the end of the Ice Age, an enormous mass of ice damned the lower part of that glen. The surface of the water was limited to the height at which the surplus water flowed over the col into the Spey – and this continued for so long that it formed a beach which now forms the parallel road.

Suggested walk

The final stretch of four miles of General Wade's road above Melgarve, is definitely only for walkers or perhaps the more intrepid mountain biker; the route beginning with a long "straight" as it climbs steadily away from the Spey, then curving into the corrie and to the base of the zigzags, and finally to the summit at 2,500 feet.

There is a logistical difficulty for anyone planning to traverse the Corrieyairack in a single day. A practical solution is to persuade a friendly driver to meet you at Melgarve – having previously dropped you off at Fort Augustus - or alternatively at Spean Bridge at a time to meet the public bus from Fort William to Inverness.

Standing stone at Coul - Dan Da Lamh in the background

Chapter 13

Dun da Lamh

Dun da Lamh is a prehistoric hill fort situated on a spectacular ridge between the Spey and the Mashie. From Laggan, the aspect is of a pointed hill, and until recently, it was simply called The Dun. The fort is well known in archeological circles, but singularly lacking in signposts or map references! Although it is 600 feet above the surrounding land, it is possible to have a very gradual ascent nearly all the way.

From the north, the motorist should leave their car at the level area near to St Michael's Chapel - immediately to the south of the Spey Dam (see Chapter 12). From here, an estate road curves round and after about half a mile, turn right, again on an estate road, gradually ascending for about a mile to a hairpin bend where the road turns on itself and continues to climb for a further mile. It is only at the roadhead that there is a signpost directing one up the final path to the fort.

The approach from the southwest is from the Laggan to Fort William road, turning right at Achduchil, and after crossing the River Mashie, turning left and following the route in the previous paragraph. Whichever way is chosen, the climb will take about 45 minutes, with the same again for the return.

Dun da Lamh means "Fort of the Two Hands" presumably reflecting its location at the end of a steep ridge between two valleys. It has been suggested that the fort dates from about 500 AD; and the fort has been described, perhaps with some exaggeration, as the most perfect specimen of a Pictish stronghold in Britain.

The wall surrounding the fort is of a most irregular shape, and encloses an area of very uneven ground extending to about an acre. The present approach is up a ramp on the west side of the fort, but it is thought that this has been constructed at a more recent time and that the original entrance would have been where there is now a gap in the north west section of the wall. The perimeter wall is incredibly broad, its width varying from 13 feet up to 23 feet. The stones of the wall are small, and it is said that all the stone, amounting to an estimated 5,000 tons, had been quarried elsewhere and carried up to the site. Ordinarily it is to be expected that the stone from such an ancient building would have been raided; but there is no evidence of this here - perhaps because of the smallness of the stone and the remoteness of the location.

The height of the wall varies considerably. To the west, the highest section of the inside of the wall is 6 feet, whereas externally, the outer face reaches a height of 9 feet on the south east elevation.

There is some indication of buildings within the fort; and also a well. Most recently, the fort was used as an observation post by the Home Guard in the 1939/45 War, and there is some evidence of this occupation in a corner to the south.

A visitor to the Fort is encouraged to chose a day with good visibility. The views are outstanding - Glen Markie to the north; to the east, Creag Dubh (Newtonmore) with Laggan in the foreground; Strath Mashie to the South; and the upper Spey valley towards the Corrieyairack in the West.

Suggested walk

If transport can be arranged, an alternative descent is to go straight on at the hairpin bend. This track gradually decends into the valley of the Pattack, and comes out near the Druim an Aird car park.

Chapter 14
Laggan Bridge to Loch Laggan

The road to Loch Laggan and on to Spean Bridge was built by Thomas Telford in 1821 – recognising that General Wade's road over the Corrieyairack was unduly mountainous and effectively seasonal.

Turning south from Laggan Church, our road crosses the Spey by a modern bridge, and across the flood plain to the junction with the road coming up from Dalwhinnie. Immediately above the junction is the farmhouse of Drumgask. Until about 1914, this building was the inn at Laggan, and a stopping place for the stage coach from Kingussie to Tulloch in Lochaber.

Half a mile beyond Drumgask, a track signposted "Dalchully" bears to the right dropping down to cross the Mashie - this track following the line of General Wade's road over the Corrieyairack. Robert Chambers, in his *History of the Rebellion of 1745* first published in 1840, narrated that when General Cope resolved to avoid the Highlanders and proceed by Ruthven to Inverness, the van of his army had reached "Blairobeg", three and a half miles south of Garvamore Inn. In John Thomson's Atlas of Scotland published in 1832, the township of "Blairagy Beg" is shown to be immediately before the crossing of the Mashie. Chambers' *History* is generally regarded as containing an accurate account of the events of this time; and it is reasonable to conclude that it was here that Cope's army indeed turned around.

Dalchully is one of the oldest houses in Badenoch. It was one of the places where Ewen Macpherson of Cluny sought refuge after Culloden, and close to the front door, there was a hidden compartment that he used. It is said that the hiding place has now been filled in.

Half a mile beyond Dalchully, one comes to the small community of Achduchil. A private road branches to the right, crossing the valley and reaching the Corrieyairack road near the Spey dam.

Continuing on the road to Kinlochlaggan, the broad strath of the River Mashie is on the right, and the road passes close to Strathmashie House, a house of particular antiquity, having been built before the 1745 Rising. On

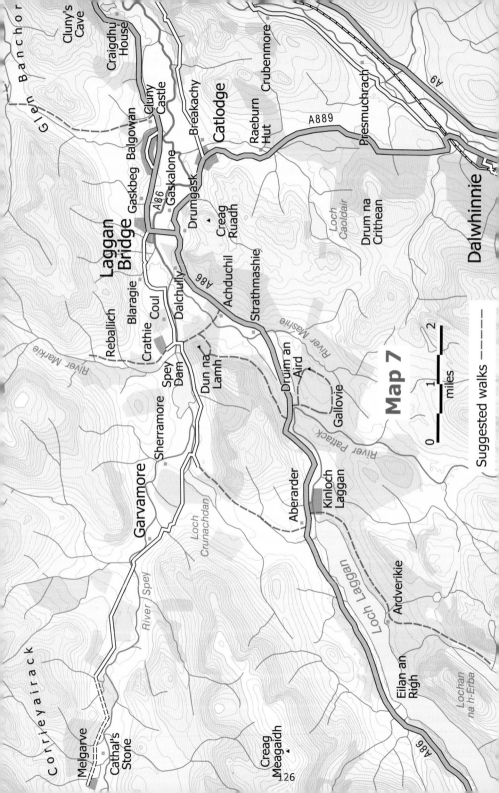

Map 7

Suggested walks

0 1 2
miles

28 August 1847, Colonel Donald McPherson entertained Queen Victoria and Prince Albert at Strathmashie House. The River Mashie is crossed by one of Telford's bridges. High up, to the left, a continuous embankment carries surplus water from the Mashie over the watershed and eventually into Loch Laggan. A gradual incline takes the road over the same watershed.

Towards the end of a long straight, the River Pattack tumbles down into a large pool by the roadside. Parking is available; and alternative paths lead to Druim an Aird, a ruined township where the foundations of the various buildings can easily be seen.

In Chapter 2, there was reference to the "Watches" that were established to counter cattle raiding. In 1725, a number of independent companies were recruited as a form of military defence force to preserve order in the districts garrisoned by them. These companies were designated *Am Freicadan Dubh* ("The Black Watch") - alluding to the appearance of their dark tartan – contrasting with the scarlet uniforms of the regular soldiers, the *Saighdearan Dearg*. In 1740, the Black Watch was formed into a regiment of the British Army as the 43rd Regiment.

Druim an Aird was the home of Corporal Malcolm McPherson of the Black Watch. When Malcolm McPherson and his fellow soldiers were recruited, it was their understanding that they would only be serving in the Highlands in the performance of a "Watch" - to protect the local communities. But in March 1743, the regiment received orders to march to London. The men were unhappy, but they were assured that it was merely to parade before the King – as he had never seen a Highland Regiment. Early in May, after they had reached London, there was a rumour that the regiment was to be sent to the West Indies. One hundred men mutinied, and under the leadership of Malcolm McPherson, they started to march north. They were intercepted; and on 19 July 1743, Malcolm McPherson and two others were shot within the Tower of London. In 2006, a memorial was unveiled in Tower Green not only to the three Highlanders but also seven others including Lady Jane Grey, Ann Boleyn and Catherine Howard, who were all executed within the Tower.

The community of Druim an Aird was reputedly abandoned after an occasion when the menfolk returning from a wedding, lost their lives in a snowstorm. The round trip to Druim an Aird (NN 573 895) is less than two miles and might take about an hour. Alternatively, a gentle stroll westwards takes one over to the Falls of Pattack. To the north (across the road), a track climbs up into the forest – and provides an alternative approach to the hill fort of Dun da Lamh.

Continuing on the road for another mile, a signpost points to a track bearing to the left and crossing the Pattack. Gallovie was at one time the name of the extensive territory extending to Loch Ericht and Ben Alder which Duncan Macpherson of Cluny ("Duncan of the Kiln") acquired from the Duke of Gordon in 1791. This track climbs over a ridge into the upper valley of the Pattack, and then on to Loch Pattack some seven miles to the south. Another track to Loch Pattack comes from Dalwinnie and Loch Ericht - providing a lengthy round trip.

A further mile down the Pattack takes the traveller to a picturesque bridge with imposing pillars and an adjacent gate-lodge – the gate-lodge having a disproportionate tower attached. This bridge gives access to Ardverikie Estate – which was established from part of the former Gallovie Estate. In 1844, Ewen Macpherson of Cluny ("Old Cluny") leased Ardverikie to the James Hamilton, 1st Marquess of Abercorn, a member of the Royal household. In the next few years, a frequent guest was Sir Edwin Landseer. (Landseer is also referred to in Chapter 8).

Lord Abercorn facilitated Queen Victoria's visit to Ardverikie in 1847. The Queen was then only 28; and it was her third visit to Scotland. In her Journal, she recorded disembarking from the royal yacht at Fort William on 21 August and proceeding by horse drawn carriage. At that time, there was no bridge over the Pattack; and before crossing on a "floating bridge", she narrated -

"Here, in spite of the pouring rain, were assembled a number of Highlanders, with Macpherson of Cluny (always called Cluny Macpherson) and three dear boys of his, Davidson of Tulloch, and others, with Lord Abercorn, in full Highland dress. We stepped out of our carriage and stood upon the floating bridge, and so crossed in two or three minutes. We then drove on, in our pony carriages, to Ardverikie, and arrived there in about twenty minutes."

She described the house, as it then was, as a "comfortable shooting-lodge, built of stone, with many nice rooms in it. Stags' horns are placed along the outside and in the passages; and the walls of the drawing-room and ante-room are ornamented with beautiful drawings of stags, by Landseer". The Queen is said to have been was delighted with Ardverikie, but it rained most of the time that she was there; and this may have caused her to settle on Balmoral!

Lord Abercorn had limited funds and the lease of Ardverikie was eventually (in 1869) acquired by Sir John Ramsden, Baronet of Huddersfield. Sir John was exceptionally wealthy; and within a short space of time, he had expended £180,000 on tree planting and other developments. This included the construction a large house, built in 1871, and rebuilt (after successive fires) in 1873 and 1878. Significantly, the original lease of Ardverikie had contained a provision that upon the tenancy coming to an end, the tenant was entitled to recompense for any improvements that might have been made on the Estate. Old Cluny had not fully appreciate the consequences of this condition. Upon Old Cluny's death in 1885, the Cluny family did not have the necessary funds to reimburse the tenant; and Ramsden was able to purchase the Estate. Indeed, it is still owned by his extended family.

It is a remarkable coincidence that Sir Compton Mackenzie, the Scottish author having published a novel in 1941 depicting life in a fictional Scottish castle of Glenbogle, and having taken as the title "The Monarch of the Glen"- a description previously given by Landseer to one of his paintings (see Chapter 8)... for the BBC in 2000 to select Ardverikie, an estate that Landseer knew so well, as the location for the series based on Compton Mackenzie's novel.

It is a pleasant walk to cross the famous bridge and proceed along the estate road towards Ardverikie; and for the more adventurous, to follow a track down the south side of Loch Laggan as far as Moy, at the south end of the Loch. And as an alternative, to bear left at the House and proceed by Lochan na h-Erba – a location featured in several programmes of the Television series.

There is a tradition that Fergus, king of Dalriada, had his hunting seat on the shores of Loch Laggan, and it perhaps significant that one of the islands in the Loch is Eilan an Righ ("the King's Island").

In 1929, an aluminium smelter was established at Fort William, powered by

Loch Laggan

Gardens at Aberarder Lodge

water from Loch Treig, and in 1934 a dam was constructed four miles west of Loch Laggan, to supplement the water supply. The reservoir behind this dam was linked to Loch Laggan by an aqueduct, and as a consequence, the level of the Loch can fall by up to16 feet in times of drought. The overall effect is to extend the magnificent sandy beach at the east end of the Loch. Over the years, the remains of several logboats have been found in the sand when the water has been low. Most of them were salvaged but the necessary treatment to preserve them was not carried out, and sadly they all disintegrated. The remaining boat was left and for some time, it could be seen underwater; but it too, has now been lost.

Returning to our road for a few yards, one comes to a fork. The track to the right leads to Aberarder Lodge, but before the Lodge, on the left, can be found a small burial ground with the ruins of St Kenneth's Church (NN 535 897). St. Kenneth (Cainnech of Aghaboe) was a distinguished Irish priest who visited Scotland with St Columba in 565 AD. He settled here and the immediate area became known as Lagan Choinnich (the small hollow, or more generally, the low land of Kenneth). The name was adopted for the whole ecclesiastical district – but the Choinnich dropped out of use, leaving the anglicised "Laggan" as we know it today.

It is said that the present church was built by a Cameron known as Allan nan Creagh. Allan was very active, and at first rather successful in levying contributions from his neighbours, and in driving off their cattle. But the tide of plunder does not always run smooth, any more than that of love. Allan, having met with some disasters in his predatory expeditions, resolved to have some communication with the inhabitants of the invisible world, in order to find out the cause. There was a celebrated witch in his neighbourhood, called Gorm Shuil, or blue-eyed. She was skilled in her profession, in that she could transform herself and others into hares and crows, raise hurricanes and perform other wonderful exploits. Under the direction of this witch, Allan went at night to a cornkiln – taking a cat with him. The cat (still living) was put on a spit; and his servant commenced the process of roasting it before a slow fire, while Allan stood at the entrance leading to the fire, with a drawn sword, to keep off all intruders. The cat wailed out doleful lamentations, and when a crowd of cats immediately gathered, Allan kept them at a respectful distance. At last, a black cat with one eye came and advised Allan that his late reverses were a punishment for his wickedness; and that, in order to atone for his guilt, and obtain forgiveness for his sins, he must build seven churches. The one-eyed cat also added that if Allan were to continue the roasting activity, the cat's brother would take summary vengeance. Allan immediately released the cat at the fire and lost no time in commencing his church building; and it is said that the old church of Laggan was one of the seven.

Prominent in the churchyard is a rectangular stone of unknown antiquity, with the outline of a cross incised into the face. In the doorway of the ruined church, there is a recess containing a font or piscina. There is a story that about two hundred years ago, a young man from Laggan was killed in an accident: his body was brought home and buried close to one wall of the church. His lover died shortly after of a broken heart, and was buried on the other side of the church. Rowan trees grew up from each grave, and entwined themselves. Sadly, there is now no trace of the graves, and the trees were hacked down for their timber late in the 19th century.

On the railings of a family plot within the burial ground, there is the following tablet -

Sacred to the memory of the members of the House of Strathmashie who repose within the west end of this enclosure. Many are the worthy names of that family, but this brief inscription must not omit Lachlan Macpherson of Strathmashie, a gentleman, a scholar and a poet who will ever be revered in his native land. This tablet, erected by the Gaelic Society of Inverness and the Clan Macpherson Association, 1998, replaces one "erected as a humble tribute of veneration and affection to their departed ancestors, by Colonel Donald McPherson, K.H., 39th Regiment and Captn. Daniel McPherson, 2nd R.V.B. - 1848".

It was Colonel Donald McPherson who had entertained Queen Victoria at Strathmashie House in the previous year.

Back on the road, at the next corner, a track on the right is the southern end of the road from Shirramore. This was at one time a "coffin road", with funerals from Crathie taking this route to reach the burial ground at St Kenneth's. The long low building on the right is the former Lochlaggan Hotel, at one time a coaching inn and a stopping point for a change of horses when the stage coach ran from Kingussie to Tulloch prior to the first World War.

In the adjacent bay of the Loch is the outlet pipe taking water from the Spey via Loch Crunachdan.

The Rev. Thomas Sinton in his *By Loch and River* (1910) related that every year, Old Cluny was in the habit of spending a day with his family at Aberarder. On these occasions, lunch was always laid out on the wooded lawns beside Loch Laggan; and boating on the loch and netting fish constituted part of the amusement of the company. There is also a record that when Andrew Carnegie spent his Summers at Cluny, he was taken fly fishing for trout on the Loch. On one such occasion, his ghillie was a young medical student from Balgowan. Carnegie was particularly interested to hear of the sacrifices necessary to pursue his studies, and it was this conversation that prompted him to establish bursaries for university students in Scotland.

Suggested walk

From the "Druim an Aird" car park, a path leads up the side of the Pattack to an impressive viewing platform from where the Pattack can be viewed coming over a series of cataracts and falling between two vertical sides into a pool below. The path then climbs over a ridge (with an alternative loop) before dropping down to a Forestry road. From here, turn right gradually climbing on to a low ridge where the outline of about ten houses can be seen... then continuing for a more direct return.

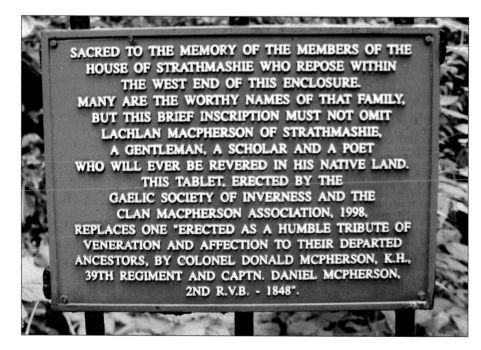

SACRED TO THE MEMORY OF THE MEMBERS OF THE
HOUSE OF STRATHMASHIE WHO REPOSE WITHIN
THE WEST END OF THIS ENCLOSURE.
MANY ARE THE WORTHY NAMES OF THAT FAMILY,
BUT THIS BRIEF INSCRIPTION MUST NOT OMIT
LACHLAN MACPHERSON OF STRATHMASHIE,
A GENTLEMAN, A SCHOLAR AND A POET
WHO WILL EVER BE REVERED IN HIS NATIVE LAND.
THIS TABLET, ERECTED BY THE
GAELIC SOCIETY OF INVERNESS AND THE
CLAN MACPHERSON ASSOCIATION, 1998,
REPLACES ONE "ERECTED AS A HUMBLE TRIBUTE OF
VENERATION AND AFFECTION TO THEIR DEPARTED
ANCESTORS, BY COLONEL DONALD MCPHERSON, K.H.,
39TH REGIMENT AND CAPTN. DANIEL MCPHERSON,
2ND R.V.B. - 1848".

St Kenneth's Churchyard

134

Chapter 15
Laggan to Dalwhinnie

This road, now known as the A889, is the first section of General Wade's road from Dalwhinnie over the Corrieyairack to Fort Augustus – commenced in 1731 and completed in the following year. Our route from Laggan Bridge to Drumgask is common with immediately preceding Chapter; but at Drumgask, we now turn left.

Over a short hill, the strange ruin of a church comes into view adjacent to a short drive leading to "The Monarch" (previously the Monarch Hotel). The steeple is still complete and the free standing walls of stone are in good condition - but that is all. In 1843, the established Church of Scotland was split asunder throughout the country; the Free Church of Scotland was formed, and in most parishes, a new "Free Church" was built whenever the breakaway congregation could secure land. Ewen Macpherson of Cluny ("Old Cluny") provided this site in 1850 and this was followed by the building of this church and the adjacent manse.

Cluny and his family supported both the established Church and this Free Church, attending the services in each church on alternate Sundays; and the respective parishioners also attended the other church if one of the ministers was not available. In 1929, many of the Free Church congregations, including the parishioners of this church, re-joined the established Church, and when the minister of this church retired in 1931, the building was sold.

There are references to Dr Isabel Grant in Chapters 2, 3 and 10. When she wrote *Everyday Life on an Old Highland Farm* in 1924, she began collecting artefacts from around the Highlands and Islands. To accommodate her growing collection, she bought in 1935 a disused church on the island of Iona. She called the museum "Am Fasgadh" ("The Shelter") because "it was to shelter homely ancient things from destruction". Within three years the Iona building was insufficient. In 1938, she took the lease of the former Free Church and manse at Laggan. Here is her description of the move from Iona-

"I had arranged for a removal firm to pack the exhibits. The men that they sent were excellent. By early October everything was crated or securely bundled together and carried down to the jetty to wait the coming of the

Ruin of Free Church at Laggan

cargo ship to which they would be taken by boat. Then gale after gale blew up. Atlantic rollers surged through the Sound. No sail could call. The stuff lay by the pier. I spent a miserable and frustrating time. At last, in early December, the ship was able to lie off the jetty and the stuff was rapidly got onboard. She was not to go directly to Oban so that I was able to go overland to Laggan to open the church and be ready to receive the collection. There had been a fall of snow. The roads were extremely slippery. The temperature inside the church was literally glacial. I planned where I would have the stuff dumped. As the day wore on I remembered all the awkward corners where on these icy roads the pantechnicon could have skidded and overturned. I got colder and colder and the early dusk fell. Finally by the light of the motor lamps the things were carried in. By now speechless, I went to Newtonmore, to Main's Hotel where Miss Main had lighted a roaring fire in my room, and she sent me straight to bed and kept me there for the inside of a week."

Dr Grant enjoyed her stay in Laggan, but her time was limited as she was largely engaged in duties associated with the War. Her ambition was for a larger site on which she could engage in traditional activities. Eventually in 1943, the local lawyer in Kingussie – Christopher Petty – told her about Pitmain Lodge in Kingussie, and it was here that Dr Grant developed her Museum – until she retired to Edinburgh in 1954.

In 1945, there was no prospective use for the church. At that time, there was an aversion to allowing an ecclesiastical building to crumble away – and accordingly, but very sadly, the roof of the church was stripped and the furnishings were burnt. The manse was renamed Gaskalone ("Gaskenloan" in John Thomson's Atlas of 1832), and from time to time, the former manse has been used as a guest house and a Hotel.

After the ruined church, the road skirts the flood plain of the Spey. High up on the right on the summit of Creag Ruadh (1594 feet) can be seen the monument to Old Cluny, chief of the Clan Macpherson from 1817 to his death in 1885. The inscription reads -

Erected by Clansmen and Friends in loving memory of Ewen Macpherson, C.B. of Cluny Macpherson, Chief of Clan Chattan, Born 24th April 1805. Died 11 January 1885.

Catlodge

There can also be seen, at a distance - on the shoulder of Creag Dhubh, a similar but smaller monument to his wife Sarah Justina.

Our road climbs and after about a mile, we come to the small community of Catlodge (*Caitleag* – the hollow of the cat) – identified in William Roy's Map of 1750 as "Catalach or Cross Hands". It is here that a branch road bears to the left and passes the farm of Breakachy – this road to be described in Chapter 17. At one time, there was an inn at Catlodge, subsequently replaced by the inn that was at Drumgask.

Across from the road junction is the drive leading to the Lodge of Catlodge. Of particular note are the small stone cats on either side of the gateway. From early times, the surrounding lands were owned by the Earls of Huntly, latterly Dukes of Gordon, and tenanted by the Macphersons of Breakachy. The Duke of Gordon evicted the Breakachy family in 1773, and the present Lodge probably dates from this period. In or about 1830, Old Cluny acquired the lands of Catlodge, and they remained in his family until the death of his last surviving son, Albert Cameron Macpherson in 1932.

In Chapter 11, the story is told of Ewen Macpherson of Cluny ("Cluny of the '45") returning home to recruit his clansmen to the Jacobite cause after the Prince had persuaded him to change his allegiance. It was at this time that the sound of the bagpipes was heard in the township of Catlodge — this was the clansmen setting out for the south, with the Green Banner unfurled. They were accompanied by their women and children as far as the Drum nan Critheann (the Aspen Ridge), the summit of the road before it drops down into Dalwhinnie. It is said that the women did nothing to hinder the departure of their menfolk, but that "a heart-rending scene took place, in the course of which they gave loud expression to their grief".

There is a tradition within the Clan Macpherson that no battle at which the Macphersons were present with the *Bratach Uiane* or Green Banner, was ever lost. The banner can now be seen within the Clan Macpherson Museum at Newtonmore.

On the right, some distance beyond Catlodge and partly obscured by scrub birch, there is a cairn to the memory of Malcolm Macpherson, "Calum Piobair", who had been piper to Old Cluny. Calum Piobair had retired to Catlodge in 1877 and lived in a cottage adjacent to the site of the present cairn. Indeed a nearby cottage is still known as "Piper's Cottage". The cairn

The plaque reads:

ERECTED BY
GLASGOW-BADENOCH ASSOCIATION
AND FRIENDS IN MEMORY OF
CALUM PIOBAIR
CALUM MACPHERSON DIED 1898
WHO HERE PRESERVED & TAUGHT THE
PIOBAIREACHD OF THE MACCRIMMONS
A MASTER MUSICIAN · A DEDICATED TEACHER

"LEANAIDH AN DIBRE IAD"

Cairn in memory of Calum Piobair

to Calum Piobair was erected in 1960, and the inscription reads -

> Erected by
> Glasgow Badenoch Association
> and friends in memory of
> Calum Piobair
> Calum MacPherson died 1898
> Who here preserved & taught the
> piobaireachd of the MacCrimmons.
> A master musician – & dedicated teacher
> "Leanaidh an oibre iad"

The cairn was unveiled by his son Angus Macpherson, himself a celebrated piper, and for many years piper to Andrew Carnegie. Calum Piobair's teaching was continued by Dr Mackay of Laggan, and in his eulogy on this occasion he observed -

"For many years after 1745, Government troops came and went on this road below us, over the Corrieyairack to Fort Augustus and Fort William, and it was their mission that the tartan should not be worn, that the people should speak their native tongue only in whispers, and that the song of the pipes should be for ever silenced. Much of our music was lost then. But over the gap are one or two slender bridges, and the road over one of these bridges leads directly from Boreraig in Skye to Laggan in Badenoch and from the MacCrimmons to Malcolm Macpherson."

Also on the roadside, there was at one time readily visible, a stone with a hollow on the top – Clach na Gruagach – the Gruagach Stone. It was the practice to leave small quantities of meal, milk or cheese as an offering to placate the spirits and ensure a good harvest.

About two miles beyond Catlodge, the road comes to a wooded area as it crosses the Allt Breakachy. On the left is a cottage, sometime known as Halfway House. The original cottage on this site was the property of Glentruim Estate; and during the 1930s it was occupied by Ian Macpherson (1905 - 1944), the novelist. His first novel *Shepherds Calendar*, was published in 1931. He wrote two more books before his final publication – *Wild Harbour*. Halfway House was rebuilt by the Scottish Mountaineering Club in 1988, and is now known as the Raeburn Hut – named after Harold Raeburn (1865 – 1926), a famous Scottish climber.

About a mile to the south west of Halfway House lies Loch Caoldair, where Calum Piobair tragically lost his life in 1898.

Our road continues, and after about three miles, drops down steeply towards Dalwhinnie – the straightness of the road reminding the traveller that this was originally a military road.

Here is Dalwhinnie Distillery, established in 1898. It was one of the first to have an overseas owner, when it was bought by an American company in 1905, but not surprisingly, the prohibition in the US caused it to be sold back to Britain. Over the years, practically all the production has gone to blending with grain whiskies, and it was only in 1988 that "Dalwhinnie" was promoted as a single malt. Notwithstanding this, 90% of the production of this distillery still goes for blending.

The area around Dalwhinnie has had a long history. The drovers who took cattle south from the Highlands, only travelled about ten miles each day, pausing in open places where their animals could have sufficient grazing to sustain them for the next day. There was such an area at Newtonmore, and Dalwhinnie provided the next stopping place before crossing Drumochter – with the open meadow at Dalnaspidal beyond: each stage being of about the preferred span. In choosing to take his road through Drumochter in 1728, General Wade recognised that the drovers had already selected the best route, and it is not surprising that a "King's House" was established at Dalwhinnie to provide sustenance and shelter for travellers. General Cope stayed here on his way north, before deciding not to confront the Highlanders coming over the Corrieyairack. Prince Charles Edward Stuart ("Bonnie Prince Charlie") also stopped here on his journey south to Edinburgh. After Culloden, Hanoverian troops were stationed here in their unsuccessful search for Cluny Macpherson. By 1770, the building was in a ruinous condition, but was restored by the Commissioners of the Forfeited Estates, who managed the lands (including the property of Macpherson of Cluny) which were confiscated after Culloden. Thereafter, many famous travellers stayed at the Inn of Dalwhinnie, as it was then known. Queen Victoria came to Dalwhinnie late on 8 October 1861, having left Balmoral that morning. She described the Inn as follows -

"...there was a drawing-room and a dining-room and we had a good sized bedroom. Albert had a dressing-room of equal size. Mary Andrews [one of her wardrobe-maids]... and Lady Churchill's maid had a room together, everyone being in the house; but unfortunately there was hardly anything to eat, and there was only tea, and two miserable starved Highland chickens, without any potatoes! No pudding, and no fun; no little maid (the two there not wishing to come in), nor our two people – who were wet and drying our and their things – to wait on us!"

Next morning was much happier -

"A bright morning, which was very charming. Albert found, on getting up, that Cluny Macpherson, with his piper and two ladies, had arrived quite early in the morning."

The building which comprised the old inn is now the southern part of the present Loch Ericht Hotel.

Dalwhinnie lies between the River Truim and Loch Ericht – but strangely this Loch drains south into Loch Rannoch and eventually into the River Tay. Even more remarkable is that as part of the Tummel Garry Hydro Electric Scheme, water from Loch an t-Seilich, at the head of Glen Tromie, is taken by tunnel and aqueduct, across the Truim and into Loch Ericht.

To the south of the railway station, a level crossing serves the private road giving access to the north east side of the Loch. The road continues for six miles to Ben Alder Lodge, and from there, a right of way continues below the slopes of Ben Alder. Sadly, sections of this path were lost when the water level was raised as part of the hydro electric scheme, but it is still possible to follow the shore of the Loch. Towards the south end of the Loch, Ordnance Survey maps identify Benalder Cottage – a disused house now used as a mountain bothy – and behind the Cottage, the maps show - "Prince Charlie's Cave". At this location, there is a large boulder under which one person might crawl; but it is not a cave, nor has it any connection with the Prince.

When Cluny Macpherson went into hiding after Culloden, he had the support of all of his clansmen. It is said that high up on the slopes of Ben Alder there was fabricated a two storey hide-out which was to become known as "Cluny's Cage". The historical record tells us that on the lower floor, built into the hillside, was a fireplace, and that the steepness of the rock behind was such that the smoke could not be seen. On the upper floor was the living area and sleeping quarters. The Prince came here in September 1746,

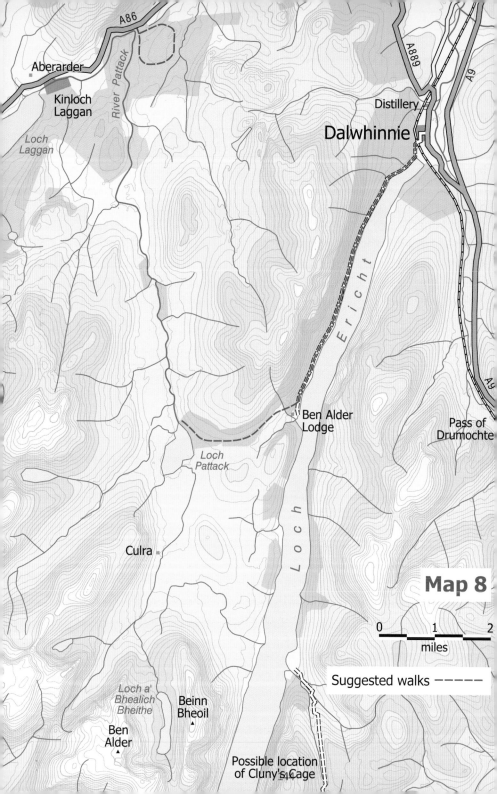

Aberarder

Kinloch
Laggan

*Loch
Laggan*

River Pattack

A86

A889

A9

Distillery

Dalwhinnie

Ericht

Ben Alder
Lodge

*Loch
Pattack*

Pass of
Drumochte

A9

Loch

Culra

*Loch a'
Bhealich
Bheithe*

Beinn
Bheoil
▲

Map 8

0   1   2
        miles

Suggested walks – – –

Ben
Alder
▲

Possible location
of Cluny's Cage

and remained in the company of Cluny for more than a week – until the Prince heard that a French ship was off the west coast – ready to take the Prince back to France. The exact location of the Cage may never be known. It may be significant that "Ben Alder" was the name given to the whole mountain range to the south of Loch Laggan. Professor Alan G Macpherson in his *A Day's March to Ruin* (1996) suggested that the Cage might have been on a steep slope above Loch a' Bhealich Bheithe which lies between Ben Alder itself and Beinn Bheoil. However, it is possible that the Cage was on the other side of Loch Ericht; and in support of this view, it is significant that in James Stobie's map of the Counties of Perth and Clackmannan published in 1783, the east side of Loch Ericht is shown as being heavily wooded, and that opposite Ben Alder there appears the words "Place where C.S. hid himself 1746", it being presumed that "C.S." referred to Charles (Edward) Stuart.

Sir Walter Scott made a relatively brief reference to the Cage in his *Tales of a Grandfather* (1829); but it was Robert Louis Stevenson in his *Kidnapped* (1886) that brought the Cage fully into literature. Much of the story is an account of the adventures of the fictional David Balfour and Alan Breck Stewart in the Highlands in 1751. In the course of their travels, David and Alan are set upon by wild Highlanders who are serving Cluny. David had been taken ill and was barely conscious. Alan convinced Cluny to give them shelter. David was tended by Cluny's clansmen and soon recovered. In the meantime Alan had lost his money playing cards with Cluny, only for Cluny to give it all back.

In this Chapter, reference has already been made to Ian Macpherson's *Wild Harbour*. In this novel (written in 1936), he foretold the onset of the Second World War and the response of Hugh and Terry, then living in Badenoch, who chose to go into hiding. Their refuge was a cave close to "Loch Coulter" which corresponds with Loch Caoldair, west of Halfway House. In describing the hide-out, it is said that it was not strictly a cave... an immense slab of rock had fallen from a precipice and had tumbled inwards to form "a long narrow tent open at both ends". There are significant differences in both the location and the description of Hugh and Terry's cave, but undoubtedly Ian Macpherson was influenced by the story of the Cage.

When the Prince left the Cage, Cluny escorted him for part of his journey to the west. On Cluny's return, he was accompanied by his clansmen back to

Badenoch. Before completing their journey, they were overtaken by darkness; and had no alternative but to sleep where they were. A watch was set - as it was known that Government troops were searching for Cluny, but, with the exception of one man, all fell sound asleep. During the night, that one wakeful man heard the galloping of horses evidently coming towards the bivouac. What was the sentry to do? Should he awaken the others? Should he let them sleep and trust that the horseman would pass? If he were to awaken the sleeping men would they be sufficiently alert and would they be able to make their preparations without some noise which would alert the searchers. Such was his dilemma. He decided to let the camp remain asleep and trust to the darkness of the night. When Cluny awakened in the morning he was told of his escape. Casting his eyes downwards to where he had lain, he saw that he had been sleeping on a clump of white heather. In thankfulness for his safety he declared that, henceforward, the badge of the Clan Macpherson would be the *Fraoch Geal* or White Heather.

Suggested walk

In Dalwhinnie, the public road to the Station turns left and ends at a level crossing. Beyond the railway, a private road leads down the lochside for six miles to Benalder Lodge, and from there to Loch Pattack. The private road is part of the right of way down the whole length of the loch and from there to Loch Rannoch; and to walk part of this road the opportunity to experience the grandeur – and the length of Loch Ericht.

Chapter 16
Dalwhinnie to Crubenbeg

Prior to the opening in 1975 of that part of the A9 which by-passes Dalwhinnie, the "Great Road North" followed the line of General Wade's road of 1728 and 1729; and it is this road that we now follow.

Passing the Distillery (which is referred to in the previous chapter), our road turns sharp right immediately after crossing the railway bridge. Glen Truim is a particularly deserted glen. Three miles beyond Dalwhinnie, there can still be made out, to the right of the road, an outline of a sheepfold and some ruins which are all that are left of the township of Presmuchrach. The railway through Glen Truim was constructed in 1863 and disused railway sleepers were always available. Some of those sleepers were used in the building of a shepherd's bothy. By 2007, it was falling into disrepair and seriously vandalised. In that year, it was moved to the Highland Folk Museum in Newtonmore and completely restored. Now within the bothy at its new site, is a display of shears and other tools formerly used by shepherds; and adjacent to the bothy is a reconstructed sheep fank.

Two miles beyond Presmuchrach, one passes the dwellinghouse of Crubenmore – named after the long low hill to the left of the road. A short distance beyond Crubenmore, a track leads to the right, crossing the Truim by a majestic two arched bridge. This bridge was built by Thomas Telford in the early 19th century, and it continued in use for about a hundred years. A short distance beyond, we also cross the Truim. (General Wade's road continued on the left bank). After half a mile, our road rises up and takes a long bend prior to crossing the railway: here there is ample parking and we may pause to take in our surroundings. On the skyline to our left are the crags of Cruban Beag, and on a lower point there is a stone which is identified on early maps as the Shepherds Cairn. Closer examination shows only initials – probably identifying a local family.

To the left of our stopping place, a narrow road leads downhill. The explorer is recommended to walk a few yards down this road for this leads to General Wade's bridge over the Truim, and the Falls of Truim - where the river charges through a maze of twisted rocks. Across the bridge, a narrow path follows the river downstream before curving up to the houses of Crubenbeg.

Wade Bridge at Crubenbeg

Falls of Truim

Immediately across the railway bridge, the motorist has no alternative but to join the dual carriageway of the A9 (completed in 1979) and speed on to Kingussie and beyond, or head back towards Perth. Between the A9 and the railway, the national cycleway heads north, following the line of road constructed in 1765 to take in a new bridge over the Spey near Newtonmore.

However, General Wade's road went straight ahead to Ruthven, six miles to the north east. In order to walk or cycle the line of this old road, one is faced with a hazardous crossing of the new dual carriageway. As a result of much local pressure, there have been some indications that there is to be a bridge or an underpass here for walkers and pony trekkers, but this may be some time ahead.

Suggested walk

To follow General Wade's road from Glen Truim to Ruthven, a practical approach is to come from the north and park at the entrance of the estate road to Etteridge. Etteridge ("Ettrish" on some older maps), and Phoines (1 ½ miles beyond) were well known for their respective Macpherson families. A mile beyond Phoines, the track turns and crosses the Milton burn. The bridge here is typical of General Wade's smaller structures, with a low arch and no parapet. A hole in the arch has been repaired with concrete, but otherwise the bridge is unchanged since it was built nearly 300 years ago. For the walker or cyclist proceeding north on this route, one has again to cross the A9 about a mile before Ruthven. On the other side of the A9, a parking bollard (!) marks the beginning of a further track that passes under the A9 and comes out to the B970 a few yards before the Ruthven car park.

Cairn in memory of Cluny of the '45

Chapter 17
Catlodge to Glentruim

This narrow road is one of the quietest in Badenoch. It is also a mystery in regard to its origins. It is certain that General Wade built roads between Fort William and Inverness (Fort George), Dunkeld and Inverness, Crieff and Dalnacardoch, and Dalwhinnie to Fort Augustus (the Corrieyairack). J B Salmond, in his Wade in Scotland (1934) concluded that he constructed some additional miles of road... but where? He particularly noted that Wade signed a Memorial on 21 November 1734 as follows-

"Now I do hereby certify that the said Wm Caulfield did this last summer repair all that part of the new road extending from Dunkeld to Fort Augustus of near 100 miles in length, as also the cross road from Garvamore to Ruthven..."

and that about the same time, a Warrant recorded -

"...Barracks of Ruthven where three of the roads lately made through the said Highlands do meet."

Salmond reasonably concluded that there was some road running parallel to the Spey, but speculated that it was a road which would correspond to the present road on the north side of the Spey from Laggan through Newtonmore – fording the Spey below Ruthven. However, this overlooks that Wade already had a road to Catlodge and a road from Crubenbeg to Ruthven - with a gap of less than five miles which would require no major river crossing. Significantly when General Cope decided in August 1745 to turn away from the Corrieyairick when his army was 3 ½ miles short of Garvamore, the accounts of what followed indicate that he remained on the south side of the Spey. William Roy's map (1747-1752) shows this road but no road on the north side of the Spey. It is therefore reasonably believed that General Wade did indeed build the road eastward from Catlodge.

Upon leaving Catlodge, the road drops down to cross the Allt Breakachy, and immediately thereafter, the farm of Breakachy on the right. Until the late 18th century, the Macpherson family of Breakachy was one of the major families of the Clan, and was closely related by marriage with the

Towards Laggan

Macphersons of Cluny. Indeed, prior to 1745, Donald Macpherson of Breakachy had married Christian, a sister of Ewen Macpherson of Cluny (Cluny of the 'Forty Five); and Donald accompanied Cluny when he entertained the Prince at the Cage in August 1746. (See Chapter 15). In regard to the next generation, Colonel Duncan Macpherson of Cluny ("Duncan of the Kiln") and Colonel Duncan Macpherson of Breakachy were both members of the British Army who fought - and were separately captured – in the American War of Independence. However, the Breakachy family never owned their lands; and in 1773 they were evicted.

The enclosed burial ground for the Breakachy family is one of the more significant structures in St Columba's Churchyard in Kingussie.

Beyond Breakachy the road gradually rises and after a little more than two miles, reaches a summit with great views over the Spey valley. Here, standing in its own enclosure, is a cairn with the following inscription -

TOUCH NOT THE CAT BUT A GLOVE

1746 - 1996

THIS CAIRN STANDS WITHIN VIEW OF CREAG
DHUBH TO COMMEMORATE THE LIFE OF EWEN
MACPHERSON OF CLUNY, COLONEL OF THE
BADENOCH MEN IN THE 'FORTY-FIVE RISING, A
SPOKESMAN AT THE JACOBITE WAR COUNCIL AT
DERBY, A LEADER AT THE SKIRMISH AT
CLIFTON IN CUMBERLAND, AT THE BATTLE OF
FALKIRK, AND IN THE ATHOLL RAID AND LAST
JACOBITE FUGITIVE TO REACH FRANCE (JUNE
1755).   CHIEF OF THE CLAN MACPHERSON
(1746-1764). BORN AT NUIDE, 11 FEBRUARY 1706,
DIED AT DUNKIRK, 30 JANUARY 1764.

"A man of extreme good sense and inferior to none in the
north of Scotland for capacity; greatly beloved by his clan;
a man not only brave in the general acceptation of the
word; but upon reflection and forethought determined and
resolute with uncommon calmness."
John Murray of Broughton

This piece of ground was generously gifted by Euan L.R.
Macpherson of Glentruim. The cairn is built of rock from
Badenoch and from all corners of the world where
Macphersons and their septs have settled.

THIS TABLET WAS UNVEILED BY SIR WILLIAM
MACPHERSON OF CLUNY AND BLAIRGOWRIE,
27TH CHIEF, ON THE OCCASION OF THE FIFTIETH
ANNUAL GATHERING
OF THE CLAN MACPHERSON ASSOCIATION
4TH AUGUST 1996

NA BEAN DON CHAT GUN LÀMHAINN

Looking above the cairn, the skyline extends from Creag Dubh westwards to the divided plateau of Creag Meaghaidh. The cleft on that plateau is known as the "Window", and it was over this route that Prince Charles Edward Stuart journeyed in August 1746 on his way to join Cluny Macpherson on Ben Alder.

A few yards beyond the Cairn, there is an open triangle with ample space for parking. Writing in 1947, the naturalist Seton Gordon related that the Ordnance Survey had placed a stone in a nearby wall to mark the actual centre of the Highlands of Scotland – the place most distant from either the North Sea or the Atlantic. Whether this is indeed the true centre depends on whether the Western Isles are taken into account, and indeed whether one includes St Kilda or even Rockall ! Claims for the centre of Scotland are also made for points near Loch Garry (south of Drumochter) and to the east of Schiehallion. The stone has long since disappeared and until recently, one could only find a cross etched into a stone on the same wall. To take matters beyond doubt, a large boulder has now been positioned on the triangle with an appropriate plaque.

At Glentruim

Continuing on our road, the mixed woodland on the left forms part of the policies of Glentruim. Until the 19th century, these lands were known as Nessintully; and indeed it was in Nessintully that Cluny Macpherson had one of his hiding places after Culloden. Early Ordnance Survey maps identify a point near to the Spey (and opposite Loch-an Ovie) with the words "Cluny's Cave". The ground is soft in this area and it is likely that this hiding place had been excavated into an embankment. Writing in 1817, Cluny's son described the place as follows -

"...but it was at Nessintully that he found the greatest quietness and security, until the cave was accidentally discovered by a trifling fellow who divulged the secret, and Cluny never afterwards occupied it. This cave was made by James Don Leslie and his brother Peter in a sequestered part of the Nessintully Wood. They only wrought at night, and all the soil was carefully put into sacks and carried to the River Spey. The inside was securely lined with deal, the roof covered over with tanned hides, over which there was some gravel, and the whole covered over with green sod. Within, there was a table, two chairs, a comfortable bed, and a press, with a small pane of glass to give light, and the whole was so ingeniously contrived and executed as to make a discovery almost impossible. Cluny never forgave the fellow that deprived him of the only comfortable lodging he had."

There is now no trace of anything unusual at this location.

Ralia is situated downstream, before the Spey bridge at Newtonmore. Ewen Macpherson of Ralia, who was born in 1782, became a wealthy man, having served as a major in the Indian Army. On retiring, he bought the lands of Nessintully and renamed them "Glentruim"; and around 1840, he built Glentruim House which still stands today. The House is not visible from this road but can be seen from the A9.

Beyond Glentruim, the road drops to cross the Truim by a substantial bridge built in 1832. Before reaching this bridge, a turning to the left leads to the caravan site known as Invernahavon. Historically, "Invernahavon" was on the other side of the Truim; and the low ground between the Truim and the Spey was the site of a famous battle in 1386. It is said that the Camerons in Lochaber had failed to pay certain rents to the Chief of the Clan Mackintosh; that the Camerons' cattle had been seized, and that they had retaken the animals. Here at Invernahavon, the Camerons were overtaken by a party from the confederation known as Clan Chattan, comprising members of the Mackintosh, Macpherson and Davidson clans. Before hostilities began, there was a dispute over seniority between the Macphersons and the Davidsons. The Macphersons stood aside. A bloody battle ensued in which the Camerons narrowly overcame the Mackintoshes and the Davidsons. A few hours later, the Macphersons belatedly joined in; and the Camerons were eventually routed. The conclusion of this feud is described in the following chapter.

Suggested walk

The open triangle near Glentruim is the point where the old military road turned south, to the bridge at Crubenbeg (referred to in Chapter 16). This three miles return makes a very pleasant walk with outstanding views to the Cairngorms. Significantly, this track has not been rutted and potholed by modern vehicles – perhaps explained by the fact that the old military roads were constructed with a sound foundation and topped with stones of decreasing size. Beyond the woods, there is a glimpse of Kingussie and the Sgoran behind Glen Feshie: and after some distance, an old signpost points to the "Right of Way to Perth Road" directing the traveller through an open field and into the small community of Crubenbeg. A road now drops down to Wade's bridge over the Truim, and then rises to the old A9 before it crosses the railway.

Chapter 18

Kingussie to Perth

The road south of Drumochter passes many places having particular interest to the student of Badenoch, and the writer makes no apology in extending this volume to cover some of these locations.

Such was the quality of the road south that in October 1729, Wade wrote to the Lord Advocate that -

"...I travelled in my coach with great ease and pleasure to the feast of oxen, which the highwaymen [his roadworkers !] had prepared for us opposite Loch Garry [ie at Dalnaspidal]; here we found four (oxen) roasting at the same time, in great order and solemnity. We dined in a tent, pitched for that purpose; the beef was excellent; and we had plenty of bumpers, not forgetting your Lord and Culloden [Duncan Forbes of Culloden, the Lord President of the Court of Session]; and after three hours stay, took leave of our benefactors the highwaymen, and arrived at the Hutt [Dalnacardoch] before it was dark."

About five miles south of Drumochter, close to Layby 70 on the southbound carriageway, is the Wade Stone - 8 feet high and 4 feet in breadth with the original inscription "1729". It is said that the stone was erected to mark the point where those working from the north met those working from the south. General Wade was particularly tall, and there is the story that he left a guinea coin on the top of the stone, returning in the following year to find that it was still there !

Turning off the A9 at Bruar, there is much more here than the present retail extravaganza. During the Rising in 1745/1746, Prince Charles Edward Stuart led his Jacobite army south as far as Derby, and then retired to the Highlands. They were followed by the infamous Duke of Cumberland. He directed Colonel Sir Andrew Agnew to take possession of Blair Castle, and similar instructions were given to position troops elsewhere in Perthshire. On 17th March 1746, Lord George Murray (the Prince's Commander in Chief) and Ewen Macpherson of Cluny secretly led a party of Murray and Macpherson clansmen in a counter-attack south from Badenoch. Lord George Murray and Cluny paused at Bruar whilst the Hanoverian troops in the various outposts were being rounded up. Agnew was alerted and led a substantial force north to meet them at Bruar. At this stage, Murray and Cluny only had about 45 men with them, and these were mostly pipers. The Highlanders spread themselves out very thinly behind a stone wall, and made such a commotion that the Hanoverian soldiers retreated to Blair Castle.

Soon after, all the successful raiding parties, with a considerable number of prisoners, reassembled at Bruar. They marched on Blair Castle and laid siege on the garrison of some 270 Hanoverians under the command of Colonel Agnew. The Highlanders had two cannon, but they were unable to make any impression on the thick walls of the Castle. A decision was then taken to starve the garrison into submission; and the Highlanders might have succeeded, but on 1st April 1746, they were summoned to return north as it had been ascertained that Cumberland was marching towards Inverness and that there would be a major battle - which, of course, took place at Culloden.

Remaining on the old road, Killiecrankie is four miles beyong Blair Atholl

In 1689, William of Orange invaded England and defeated King James II (James VII of Scotland) at Monmouth. James fled to France; and the Scottish Parliament voted to give the crown of Scotland to William and his wife Mary (a daughter of James). In response, James Graham of Claverhouse, Viscount Dundee ("Bonnie Dundee") raised a Highland army against the newly installed monarch. This army included a party of Macphersons from Badenoch, and Rob Roy Macgregor. A Scottish government army under General Mackay was raised to counter the rebellion. On 27th July 1689 General Mackay came through the Pass of Killicrankie and was heading for Blair Castle when the Highlanders attacked. The Highlanders routed Mackay's army; but Claverhouse, was killed; and a stone in a field marks the place where he fell. This stone is to the left of the road, clearly visible in the middle of a field about half a mile before the village of Killlcrankie. With the death of Claverhouse, the Highlanders became disheartened, and three weeks later they were defeated at Dunkeld.

On the north side of Perth, as one approaches the city centre, there is a large area of open parkland known as the North Inch. At the end of the previous chapter, reference was made to the battle of Invernahavon in 1386. For ten years after that date two of the clans were involved in a bloody feud which distressed even the king, Robert III. In desperation, he ordered each of the clans to nominate thirty of their brave men to fight it out on the North Inch. The identity of the respective clans remains an open question to this day. In the ancient documents, there are references to both "Clan Kay" and "Clan Quhele". It has been suggested that one of these participants was the Clan Chattan; but the Clan Chattan was never more than a confederation of the Mackintoshes, Macphersons, Shaws, Davidsons and others: and as may be seen from the account of the battle of Invernahavon, the constituent clans were already going their separate ways. It is believed that it was the Clan Macpherson which constituted the Clan Chattan in narrative accounts of the battle of North Inch. But who was the other party? Some writers have speculated that the Clan Cameron was involved; but the likelihood is that the other party was the Clan Davidson - which had fallen out with Clan Macpherson even before hostilities began at Invernahavon.

In 1638, Henry Adamson published a history of Perth in verse entitled *Muses Threnodie: of Mirthful Mournings on the death of Mr Gall*, and in this volume he describes the battle of the North Inch of Perth in 1396 as follows -

...that cruel bloody fead [feud],
Between these cursed clans Chattan and Kay,
Before King Robert John upon the day,
Appointed then and there, who did convene,
Thirty 'gainst thirty matched upon that greene.
But upon finding that one man was
missing from the ranks of Clan Chattan,
there... was found at length,
One Henry Wind, for tryal of his strength
The charge would take, a sadler of his craft,
I wot not well, whether the man was daft.
For an half French crown he took in hand,
Stoutly to fight so long as he might stand.
......

None fought so fiercely, nor so well deserved
As this their hired souldier, Henrie Winde
For by his valour, victory inclined
Unto that side...

Sir Walter Scott, in his *The Fair Maid of Perth* (1828) describes the competing affections for Catharine Glover (the "Fair Maid") and in particular by Henry Gow or Smith, otherwise known as Hal of the Wynd; and it is believed that Henry Adamson's verses were the source of Sir Walter Scott's account of the Battle of the North Inch, which comes into his story before Henry ultimately marries Catharine. Scott gives a fictional account of the Battle, and towards the climax, he records -

"The two pipers, who, during the conflict, had done their utmost to keep up the spirits of their brethren, now saw the dispute well nigh terminated for want of men to support it. They threw down their instruments, rushed desperately upon each other with their daggers, and each being more intent on despatching his opponent than in defending himself, the piper of Clan Quhele was almost instantly slain and he of Clan Chattan mortally wounded. The last, nevertheless, again grasped his instrument, and the pibroch of the clan yet poured its expiring notes over the Clan Chattan, while the dying minstrel had breath to inspire it. The instrument which he used, or at least that part of it called the chanter, is preserved in the family of a Highland chief to this day, and is much honoured under the name of the *federan dhu* or black chanter."

Successive chiefs of the Clan Macpherson were the proud possessors of the Black Chanter until Cluny Castle was sold. The Chanter is now on display at the Clan Macpherson Museum in Newtonmore.

Finally, it should be mentioned that Scott's novel was in turn the inspiration for Georges Bizet's opera *La jolie fille de Perth*, in which the principal characters are Henri Smith and Catherine Glover.

Bibliography

By Loch and River (1910) — Thomas Sinton

Captain John Macpherson – A Counter-blast (1900) — Alexander Macpherson

Circuit Journeys (1888) — Henry, Lord Cockburn

The Chiefs of the Clan Macpherson (1947) — W Cheyne-Macpherson

The Clans, Septs and Regiments of the
Scottish Highlands (4th Edition 1952) — Frank Adam

Creag Dhubh (1949 – 2015) — Journal of Clan Macpherson Association

A Day's March to Ruin (1996) — Alan G Macpherson

Everyday Life on an Old Highland Farm (1924) — Dr Isabel Grant

Glen Feshie (2005) — Meryl M Marshall

Glimpses of Church and Social Life
in the Highlands(1893) — Alexander Macpherson

A Highlander Looks Back (1953) — Angus Macpherson

Highways and Byways in the Central Highlands (1947) — Seton Gordon

History of the Munros of Fowlis (1898) — Alexander Mackenzie

History of the Rebellion of 1745 (1840) — Robert Chambers

In the Glens Where I Was Young (1988) — Meta Scarlett

In the High Grampians (1948) — Richard Perry

Kidnapped (1886) — Robert Louis Stevenson

Kingussie and the Caman (1994) — John Robertson

Kingussie and Upper Speyside (6th Edition 1910)
Published by — George A Crerar, Kingussie

Laggan's Legacy (2000) — Laggan Heritage

Laggan Past and Present (1990) — Dr Ian Richardson

Legends of Badenoch (1965) — Published by J Johnstone, Kingussie

Legends of the Cairngorms (1987) — Affleck Gray

Leaves from the Journal of our Life
in the Highlands (1868) — Queen Victoria

A Look at Invereshie (c1994) — Sarah Fraser Nisbet

The Making of *Am Fasgadh* (2007) — Patrick Grant

Memoirs of a Highland Lady (2nd Edition 1911) — Elizabeth Grant

More Leaves from the Journal of our Life
  in the Highlands (1885) — Queen Victoria

Old Grampian Highways (1977) — John Kerr

Perth and North Thereof   (1966) — George T Hay

The Poetry of Badenoch (1906) — Thomas Sinton

The Posterity of the Three Brethern
  (5th Edition 2004) — Alan G Macpherson

Romantic Badenoch (1904) — Published by J Johnstone, Kingussie

Scotch Missed (2000) — Brian Townsend

Scotland's Road of Romance (1934) — Augustus Muir

Stells, Stools, Strupag (2007) — Campbell Slimon

Recollections of a Speyside Parish (1888) — James Thomson

Romance of the White Rose (1933) — Grant R Francis

Wade in Scotland (1934) — J B Salmond

Wild Harbour (1936) — Ian Macpherson

Index of Place Names in Badenoch